Praise For Dick Bentley's Books
"Post-Freudian Dreaming"
and
"A General Theory Of Desire"

Updike on Acid.... Trip out with Dick Bentley. He can take you far out and then surprise you by evoking ordinary life and feeling so unerringly. Flashbacks guaranteed.
    Diane Lefer *The Circles I Move in, Radiant Hunger*

What intelligence, what fun!
    Pamela Painter *Getting to Know the Weather, Wouldn't You Like to Know*

Line after line leaped out at me, sometimes elegant as Fred Astaire, sometimes like a monkey mugging with huge teeth.
    Sharon Sheehe Stark *The Dealer's Yard, A Wrestling Season*

Bentley has really first-rate imagination. At times playful, at times darkly satiric, at other times empathetic, it's a talent that continually illuminates his work.
    W. D. Wetherell Autumn, *A Season of Discovery, Hills Like White Hills*

Wide-raging romps that bear an avid, wry curiosity about the world and its ways, a willingness to look a quarter turn to the quirky for answers, and a consistent, quiet grace of language.
    Bonnie Wells, *Hampshire Gazette*

It is the poet's voice --- inquisitive, edgy at times, tender at other times --- that gathers these poems together. It is a voice both innocent and lacerating.
    Clare Rossini Lingo, *Winter Morning with Crow*

Innovative, fresh, quirky, and wise.
    Pat Schneider *How the Light Gets In, Long Way Home*

The title refers to a thesis that humankind is entering a Post-Freudian dream world where dreams actually mean something and are accompanied by graphs, charts, and equations. Bentley woke up screaming from this dream, and presumably continued writing the pieces for this incisive collection.
    Christopher Rand *Making Democracy Safe for Oil*

Acclaim For "All Rise"

Summaries Of The Stories In This Book by Bob Hawley
Writing for the Fun of It.

Shrine:
Once again Bentley confronts the most elemental questions: Who am I? What am I doing here? Now? Why me? Is there anybody else in my world? Infused with the verbal iconography that takes us directly to the Madonna confronting the crucified Jesus and reinvents the whole birth-agony-death of "Our Savior" in a new contemporized context. Our Madonna, unnamed in this piece, is with child of uncertain fatherhood, and she, staring into the face of the Almighty, compels us with her suddenly to perceive a new reality.

Not There, They're Not:
In a sparse 1500 tale, Bentley recounts one major battle in the ongoing and eternal War Between the Sexes, where male wit, bravado, and weighty erudition is once again foiled by the wily ambuscade of one lone Amazon. This is a tasty morsel of smoked oyster on a multi-grain cracker, short, short, urging us for more.

Two Birds, One Stone:
The Garden of Eden reconstituted here as The Greenery, a pick-up bar in Boston's Faneuil Hall, where our Adam spies his erstwhile Eve enticing her new victim. But wait, who is the victim here as our Adam wears his private dream on his loosened necktie, where we read hope, passion, despair. The former couple—are they a couple? Could they still be a couple? Will they ever really be a couple? Or are they a couple, never to be again? Bentley deftly plucks our inner harp. We laugh, We hope, We cry.

The Director:
Like a nested Russian doll within a nested Russian doll, within a nested Russian doll, Bentley reveals the inner thoughts beneath the inner thoughts beneath the inner thoughts of one woman applicant seeking a place for her young child in the favored nursery school. She is one of life's victims of the Fear of Success, where at the very heart of fear is the ghostly presence of The Male Decider, the final gate-keeper beyond whose barrier none of the female sex can ever pass.

~

With a strong sense of disorientation that features our time, Richard Bentley conjures up in his stylish short stories a world that aptly reflects the absurdity of our own. All the characters seem to get lost either physically or mentally. In "Shrine" an addled teenage heroine climbs up a maintenance ladder on a mysterious structure ("The World's Biggest Crucifix") which she and her friends discover on a ski trip. Like a sleepwalker, she suddenly finds herself high and hanging up on a ladder. She then looks up and realizes that, although she can almost see the face, she finds it "dark and snowy." This nebulous description of the surrealistic structure, like Kafka's illusory castle, is the theme of the story. Is it an incarnation of the God or some unapproachable, vicious power with a vitriolic face. All the characters in these remarkable stories and poems explore the meaning of life and search for answers in their own bizarre and achingly funny ways.
    Xiaoda Xiao
    The Cave Man,
    The Visiting Suit, Stories from my Prison Life

Dick Bentley has a keen sense of the humorous. He cuts-out figures of individuals with a sharp, straight-edged tool, but his vision is always focused on the inner person.
    Peter Schneider

The illustrations and graphic poems in
"*All Rise*" can be viewed in full color
on the author's website

www.dickbentley.com

For a full picture of graphic poetry, its practice in education,
in art, and literature, please visit the author's Facebook page

www.facebook.com/BooksbyDickBentley

Fadeout

A patch of sun

leaves the leaf world
greenly dim

the dank eyelid

of sunset

closing

For Davey
with hugs, smiles, secret handshakes,
and the dreams we all share

Acknowledgments

The author thanks the following
magnificently innovative and avant-garde publications
where these works first appeared,
sometimes in different versions and under different titles.

Literary Magazines and Journals:

Alaska Quarterly Review
Argestes
Battered Suitcase
Binnacle
Blueline
Brink Magazine
Broken Plate
Chaffey Review
Chicago Review
Chrysalis
Descant
DosPassos Review
Fiction Week
Hayden's Ferry Review
Hurricane Review
Iodine Opencut
Karamu
Louisiana Review
Louisville Review
Mississippi Crow
Nimrod
North Atlantic Review
Pacific Review
Painted Bride Quarterly

Paterson Literary Review
Permafrost
Pine River Papers
POEM
Poet Lore
Red Cedar Review
River Oak Review
RiversEdge
Slant
Slow Trains
Social Register Observer
Stringtown
Tar Wolf Review
Texas Review
Under Wraps
West Wind
Xavier Review
Yale Record
xyz

Anthologies and Collections:
Cadillac Cicatrix
Main St. Rag Anthology
Pig Iron Press
Fulcrum Annual
Writing Disorder Anthology
Meridian
Best Fiction of 2012
Paris Review/ Writers Workshop – Fiction Award

International Journals
Fire (UK)
Lamport Court (U.K.)
Paris Transcontinental (France)
Pense Aqui (Brazil)
Tremblestone (U.K.)

pelorian digital
One Front Street
Leeds, Massachusetts
01053 USA

www.pelorian.com

All Rise
Copyright © 2014 by Dick Bentley
Cover and Interior design by Richard Rasa
Front Cover graphic by Faith Seddon, Dick Bentley and Richard Rasa
Graphic Poem Design by Faith Seddon and Dick Bentley
Rodin Panel Photography by Dick Bentley
Rodin Panel Graphic Design by Richard Rasa

All rights reserved. This book may not be reproduced in whole or in part, or transmitted in any form, without written permission from the publisher, except by a reviewer who may quote brief passages in a review, nor may any part of this book be reproduced, stored in a retrieval system, or transmitted in any form or by any means electronic, mechanical, photocopying, recording, or other, without written permission from the publisher.

ISBN-13: 978-0692226919
ISBN-10: 0692226915

ALL RISE
DICK BENTLEY

Contents

The Director ~~~~~~ 5
Newspaper ~~~~~~ 8
Messenger ~~~~~~ 9
Out of the Attic (A part of the house where your life is or was - isn't or wasn't) ~ 10
Flash (Teenagers search for love, laughter and integrity in random order) ~~~~ 12
At the Aquarium ~~~~~~~~~~~~~~~~~~~~~~~~~~~~~~~~~~~~~~ 24
Each Petal Is Perfect~~~~~~~~~~~~~~~~~~~~~~~~~~~~~~~~~~ 25
Overcoats (Ghost of Gogol invades Writers' Conference)~~~~~~~~~~~~~~ 26
Shrine (Less-than-virginal Madonna faces her Almighty)~~~~~~~~~~~~~ 35
Accomplice (Will they bond, or is it a limited partnership?) ~~~~~~~~~~~ 38
Layoff ~~~~~~ 41
Landlocked ~~~~~~ 42
La Porte de l'Enfer ~~~~~~~~~~~~~~~~~~~~~~~~~~~~~~~~~~~ 44
Two Birds, One Stone (Divorced couple reunites in a singles bar) ~~~~~~~~ 57
Between My Finger and My Thumb ~~~~~~~~~~~~~~~~~~~~~~~~ 68
Carpathians ~~~~~~ 69
Earth Rising ~~~~~~ 71
Onlooker ~~~~~~ 72
A Place Where You're Known ~~~~~~~~~~~~~~~~~~~~~~~~~~~~ 73
Snowstorm in Eden ~~~~~~~~~~~~~~~~~~~~~~~~~~~~~~~~~~~~ 74
Cheerful Authority ~~~~~~~~~~~~~~~~~~~~~~~~~~~~~~~~~~~~ 75
Ants ~~~~~~ 76
Christmas in Amherst ~~~~~~~~~~~~~~~~~~~~~~~~~~~~~~~~~~ 77
Dec. 6, 1984 ~~~~~~ 78
In the Cafétéria ~~~~~~~~~~~~~~~~~~~~~~~~~~~~~~~~~~~~~~ 79
Leaving Chicago (memoir fragment) ~~~~~~~~~~~~~~~~~~~~~~~~ 80

Lines Composed Upon the Brooklyn Bridge After an All-nighter	83
The News	84
Promised Land (Growing up in Queens)	85
Read Rage	92
Not There They're Not (Nightclub stripper-mom further fuels the sex wars)	93
This can't be Sunday	97
Sugaring	98
Odd Ode	99
Sometimes I Get Angry	100
Liver	101
Barista	102
Tuesday at Ten (health insurance)	103
Liberal Fascism	104
Bears on the Street, a Stockmarket pastoral	105
Woman on an Island	106
Strident Light	107
For Felony, a Departed Cat	108
Lifting Snowfall	109
Scissors Confiscated in an Airport Line	110
Halloween Afternoon	111
this great demand	112
Mockingbird	113
Bobby Bear Ruins A Picnic	114
Bunny	116
Up North	121

The Director

I'm trying not to make too much out of our encounter. I'm dressed competently, casually. No high heels. No jewelry. Everything is calculated so that the Director won't think I'm trying to impress her. The receptionist offers me a comfortable chair. I open James's file—how can a five-year-old have such a thick folder already? I keep my head down, eyes on the pages. I listen to the chatter in the outside office, trying to pick up any insider information about the school to mention during the interview. Feel smart. Feel organized.

Now I'm alone with the director in her office, and I think we might have a special rapport. She's about my age, maybe a few years older.

Actually, much older.

But we could become friends, I hope. We could develop a special rapport. That would be so important. She might think, considering me thoughtfully, "Here is an intelligent woman like myself. Here is a woman who's not trying to impress me, who wants me to treat her as an equal. She's quiet, not aggressive. She sits there, very composed, holding her child's application file. I can tell she's appealing, quite intelligent, and will be interesting to talk to."

That's what I'm hoping she will think.

And now, here she is, the director of the school, meeting with me face to face and with no distractions.

No one is coming in and out of the room. This is not like my workplace, where we all have to sit around a table to perform and to summarize our reports briefly and crisply and self-servingly. No one here will interrupt with a question I haven't anticipated or ask a question so ridiculous I will inadvertently snicker and roll my eyes, offending not only the questioner but everyone else in the room as well.

She, the director, is telling me the school has very stringent tasks, goals, and objectives that are required of all children. I nod. These tasks, goals, and objectives are quite challenging for children of any ability-grouping or age level. I should be quite satisfied if my child were able to perform—given the opportunity—at the average level. I nod again and smile.

But now the Director is suddenly railing at me. She wants to know why I think my child is gifted? Gifted? Did I say that? I don't think I would have been so politically naïve as to say "gifted." But James is certainly a gifted child, according to all I've seen and read.

She's swarming all over me, but in a quiet, precision-bombing manner. She's even smiling. I will take a deep breath, disappear under the surface, come back up for air, and try to say something.

She is discussing limbic resonance. This is the most important commodity to provide for children. Far more important than whether they are gifted.

What is limbic resonance? I'm glad you asked. So glad you asked. It is the symphony of mutual exchange and internal adaptation whereby two mammals—such as you and your child—become attuned to each other's inner states. Eye contact, for example…when we meet the gaze of another, two nervous systems are achieving a palpable and intimate apposition.

She glares at me to illustrate her point. She says it's like the wordless harmony between lovers holding hands in a restaurant, between a boy and his dog, or between a mother and a child. Yes, a mother and a child, as well as a teacher and a student.

Is it like love?

Yes, she says, it is like love. She says that parents who contemplate staying at home to raise children are treated to a cultural chorus of well-meaning dissuaders, who tell them they're bright, they're talented, and should be doing something with their time besides raising a child. The implication is clear. Love doesn't accomplish anything. Love does nothing that society needs to have done. So we, people like me, the director says, give our children over to daycare and schools like hers because our culture automatically equates full-time parenting with the absence of ambition.

She smiles smugly, proud of her self-criticism.

On one hand, she says, conservatives dismantle welfare so that single mothers must set children aside and return to work—not the labor of raising children, but the real work our culture values upholds, such as folding dresses at Wal-Mart, acquiring exalted titles, glamorous friends, exotic vacations, washboard abs, designer everything. Liberals, on the other hand, champion child care initiatives calling for an expansion of institutionalized surrogate care. She's ripping along here, enjoying her sarcasm about Wal-Mart. She is speaking slowly and calmly and I haven't the slightest idea what this has to do with James, but I'm trying to look attentive. Either way, she says, between these extremes, our children are doomed— doomed because Americans have grown too used to the efficiencies of modern life such as microwave ovens, laser price scanners, number crunching computers, high-speed internet access. Why should relationships be any different? Shouldn't we be able to compress them into less time? Give our children over to institutions?

With my shaky voice, I try to say something intelligent, but now she's doing her best, trying to remember her manners. After all that lecturing, she's not the one to discuss gifted children. She can't help me.

But I never said my child was gifted.

Never mind. You implied it. Now she stands up and sticks her hand across the desk. It flutters like a bird of prey. I'm supposed to shake it and leave.

I wonder if the director has a husband. What an impossible thought! What would he be like?

He'd poke his head in the door while we're talking. "Sorry, honey, I didn't know you were with someone."

Or maybe he'd call her "baby doll."

But he would make no attempt to excuse himself, step back, or close the door. He would look at her fixedly, taking note of me, however.

"Having a rough day? You should come home."

What a sweetheart he is. How does he put up with her?

But perhaps I've missed his meaning.

Outside it has started to rain. The rain makes needles against the window pane. The Director is standing beside him now, at the window.

She's ready to break into tears at any minute. He strokes his chin. He's got to put on a good face for my sake.

Her breathing slows. She says nothing. She knows, or thinks she knows, where this is leading. She passes a hand over her eyes, then walks back to her desk and sits down with a sigh. She's proud. She's never asked for anything in her life.

The husband looks at his wife as a man would look at a coffee urn or a pile of stones.

He turns to me, "So sorry to subject you to all of this. My wife would like to offer her sincerest apologies."

He looks at his watch. "You have an appointment tomorrow at the next school. Be kind. Be generous in the way that my wife was not kind and generous with you."

His eyes dance away for a moment, then back to me. "Look your best," he says. "Wear high heels. Wear lots of jewelry. Wear your hair streaked and upswept as only you can wear it."

Newspaper

Open to me, says the world,
speaking in such clear-cut sentences
that I see beauty in its style.

I stand at the doorway,
Ridiculous in pajamas.
What others find in art, I find in news.
What others find in human
love, I find in news, so very trouble-free.

Sunrise, a smaze of dampness
over every growing thing,
beads of cold light
formed on the orange wrapper.
Is there a voice here?

Open to me, says the world,
so that I can finally say
tomorrow and the day after and even
the future. News, the hailer, the healer,
the tutor --- more than beauty.

Death cannot harm me,
more then the news stirs me,
my cherished life.

Messenger

A bird flies into our kitchen.
It's a mistake, there's
no open window, no one's
come or gone
through the back door.
Something from down the chimney?
Who knows—it just sits
by the table leg, wings spread,
breast heaving. You try
to slide a dustpan under the bird,
with brown paper bag poised above it,
in case it takes off
—and—
it flutters away, lands next to the fridge.
I notice, you know.
Who could send such a lightweight
to deride our patience?

We could have had rhapsodies
instead of this messenger,
that tells us you are my life's biggest grievance,
and I use you,
and I require you.
What I am not
rises like sorrow between us.

Out Of The Attic

They took down the Italian Christmas lights that had shone in their window for 35 years. They coiled them carefully and placed them in one of the plastic garbage bags.

They looked at the cardboard boxes marked "SAVE" and decided not to open them. They could be thrown out, too.

They threw out empty boxes that contained Styrofoam shapes for the electronic equipment that had come in them.

Very little sentimental value here, Seth said.

Emily didn't laugh but smiled slightly when they came across a box containing 25 pairs of Dr. Scholl's wooden sandals. Emily and a neighbor had bought them on spec 15 years before, when the company went out of the sandal business. They were excellent sandals, but Emily and the neighbor had not gotten around to selling them to their friends at the slightly inflated prices they had anticipated.

When in doubt, throw it out, Seth said.

Emily looked at a box of shoulder pads. Were they for football or for baseball? She saw the line of hockey sticks of varying lengths in a corner. The boys had never been particularly athletic, she recalled. How had they managed to acquire all this equipment? The skis and boots and poles. Throw it all away.

They threw out a poster of Mao Tse Tung which depicted the U.S. Capitol Building in Washington in flames. One of their sons had hung it in his college room.

They threw out skates, rubber boots, board games, Ping-Pong paddles.

The new place would never hold even a fraction of all these belongings. But it was acceptable. There was a library and a small exercise room. They had a bridge club and a current events discussion group. There was a small garden outside the dining hall where people could sun themselves.

They stacked up two small decks and four tiny wooden chairs for the scavengers.

As they worked, Seth became aware of the mountainous and deadening accrual of habit that had burdened their lives.

When in doubt, throw it out, he said again, but without cheer.

Emily thought of their years together, how the common secret of marital contempt was hard, at times, to restrain—the instinct to flee, to hide. In many respects it was the deepest trunkful of all. Best to throw it out as well.

They threw out hatboxes with 1940s hats in them. A legacy. They threw out a box of doll's clothing along with five naked dolls and their daughter's stuffed animals, one of them a rhinoceros. They threw away letters that

Seth had received from a fictional Cocker Spaniel when he was a child. They dumped out boxes of letters and postcards from family members they had never met, some dating back to 1918.

They would show strength. They would dispense with sentiment. Nostalgia was not a factor now. They would carry on. Next, they would attack the second floor, then the first floor, then the basement.

They looked at an old, crimped photograph of a bride holding a bouquet. Neither of them could identify her.

After the basement, finally would come the move, the move to the place with the garden and all the people sitting quietly in the sun.

Flash

We called him Flash because he came and went like a caped superhero; he was a different person each day and his personality changed according to where he was. He could never sit still. He loved to light matches. He always had a box of matches, kitchen matches, and he'd light one right after another and they'd flare up. He would hold the match under his chin, make a face, and then drop it onto the tar paper of the roof where we sat.

Flash and I would sit like that in the thick, warm darkness, our faces illumined by the occasional match flicker. He was easy to joke with. He enjoyed hanging out with us girls, and he never stopped being in love with Jane even though she'd tell him again and again that she only saw him as a friend. She'd be going out with Jason or David or whoever and Flash and I would sit together on the roof of Jane's garage making grand plans of romance for ourselves. That was the summer I liked Max Huddle. Becky and Jane would go with their boyfriends to the attic or down to the cornfield behind the house, and Flash and I would always end up together, feeling like losers, but glad to have each other's company.

Jane's house was farther out in the country than most of ours. When we sat on the garage roof at night, we could sometimes see a hulking machine that growled in the distance, rumbling up and down the rows of corn with its single headlight skimming over the tops of the stalks. On the road in front of the house, passing bikers would beep a greeting at the owner of the motorcycle shop across the street. The high street lights threw leafy shadows across the lawn, and we could sometimes hear the sound of a distant train over the clatter of crickets.

"Shannon," Flash would say, "Why do you like Max Huddle? You're too good of a girl for Max Huddle." Then he'd strike a match for emphasis, hold it under his chin, and make a frowny face with the corners of his mouth turned down. He'd laugh, drop the match on the roof, and reach for another. On the subject of Jane, he lacked this kind of perspective. Flash would talk about Jane's hair—"auburn," "shimmering." He would talk about Jane's nose and Jane's slender ankles. Had I ever noticed how small Jane's fingers were, or had I seen the way she bit her lip when asking a question? It's surprising, I guess, that we didn't burn the garage down.

Our whole group ate a lot of Popsicles that summer, resting on Jane's screened-in back porch and flipping through old magazines or through an enormous paperback version of *Changing Bodies, Changing Lives*. Jane's mother had given it to her when Jane turned 13, and we'd spend hours examining the diagrams or reading aloud especially juicy passages. The personal story we loved best of all was by a boy who said he got turned on when he heard the hum of vacuum cleaners. We memorized this passage and recited it to each other. Once when we were saying the lines, we were eating spaghetti, and Flash laughed so hard his face went down toward the plate and when he drew in his breath a noodle shot up his nose. We wouldn't have felt comfortable joking about this stuff with other boys. Only with Flash.

One afternoon we washed the inside of Jane's garage, and we started splashing water at each other. I grabbed a bucket and dumped its contents on Flash, sloshing the liquid onto his head so it dripped through his dark, dry hair and in streams down his face. The bucket didn't just hold water, though, there was also turpentine in it, and I burned him, and he had to ride his bike home in sopping, stinging clothes. But he never got mad at me. That's the way Flash was.

We first met late one night by the cornfield at the bottom of the hill behind Jane's house. Jane and Becky were smoking, and though I didn't smoke, I'd gone along with them. We noticed two figures creeping through the cornstalks, and we became silent. One of the figures tripped and cursed, and when we heard his voice it was obvious it wasn't that of an adult. "Hey," Becky called. "Who's there?" The person who responded, the clumsy one, was Flash. The other guy was Kevin Stansfield, and they told us they were cutting through the field on their way to a high school party. That's how cool they were. We were so impressed we invited them up to the house.

Jane's parents had gone out again, and the five of us sat in her kitchen, trying to be witty. In the light, Kevin was the better looking of the two. I could tell that Becky and Jane already liked Kevin, but I thought he was a jerk. They knew a lot of the same kids that we did, and Kevin would cut down on most of them in such a way that he made whatever he said seem kind, as if he knew some real dirt but he was such a good guy that he wouldn't blast their reputations. Later that night, after the boys had gone to the party and then returned to Jane's house, Becky fooled around with Kevin, and she'd get together with him from time to time for the rest of the summer, but I never saw him again, which was fine with me. I didn't like the way he constantly mentioned drugs or how, when Becky told him about my obsession with Max Huddle, he said, "Yeah, I know Max. Hey, Flash, he's the guy who Ernie beat up last week, right?"

Flash was different. He also knew Max, and thought it was hysterical that I'd met Max at dancing school at our country club. He asked me which had made my heart melt, Max's talent with the fox trot or the waltz, and then he gave a demonstration of the way he pictured us dancing, which consisted primarily of banging his head against the refrigerator and hugging himself so that it looked like another person was caressing his back.

Kevin didn't return to Jane's after that night, but Flash did, never calling before he showed up but merely gliding into the driveway on his skateboard or his bike, and pretty soon he was there as often as Becky and I were.

We saw Flash nearly everywhere that summer after eighth grade. We'd be at the Snackmart in Whistler Square, sitting at a table and drinking milkshakes, and he would walk in the door grinning hugely. The manager of the Snackmart didn't like teenagers, especially boys, because they skateboarded in his parking lot, slamming across the pavement by the gas pumps and skidding close to the station wagons full of children who whined for ice cream cones. We would sip our shakes as slowly as possible, and if the manager was giving us the eye, Becky would start smoking just to piss him off a little more.

Flash was the youngest kid in his family. He had a way older brother named Joel, and, though I never saw him, Jane said he was the only one of the children who really looked half black. Joel was the drummer in a band, and a while back he'd gone to California to look for their father. He never found him, but he met a girl named Sunny. Flash had seen her only once and told us she had eyes like blossoms, whatever that meant, but that she was a spider of a woman—a trapper, he meant. Early the previous fall, Joel had sent the message that Sunny was pregnant. In June, they named the child Damon Ray, and Flash would go around Jane's house muttering, "Damon Ray. Did you hear that? Damon Ray. Is it a girl? A boy? Both? Damon Goddamn Ray."

Flash also had an older sister named Theresa. She was pretty in a tangled-up sort of way. Her hair was bushy and curly, and she wore long skirts and read poetry. Flash sometimes quoted, "Let us go then, you and I, / when the evening is spread out against the sky . . ." He was good at memorizing and if he wasn't driving me crazy with annoying lyrics from various commercials, he'd recite poetry, practicing for when he'd woo Jane. I assumed Flash had written the poems, and once, feeling generous, I suggested he show some of them to his teacher; a couple weren't too bad. He looked at me peculiarly and said, "They aren't by me." I took that to mean that Theresa was the author, and for a long time I didn't know differently. After all, Theresa was the kind of girl who would in banal, ordinary conversations use the word "vagina." Jane and I thought, though we never said it to Flash, that Theresa would be an ideal person to share her thoughts with the editors of the next edition of *Changing Bodies, Changing Lives*.

Flash's mother owned a store on Hyde Avenue called Witch's Cauldron. They sold clogs and tie-dyed clothing and silver jewelry melted into the shapes of snakes or peace symbols, and they burned so much incense it was difficult to breathe in there. Usually, the other customers glared at us, and Theresa, if she was working in the back, would tap her black fingernails against the cash register and, gesturing toward Jane and Becky and me, tell Flash to make the preps leave. Flash's mother was nicer than that and was more normal than we expected. She invited us to dinner once, and we sat at their kitchen table eating lasagna and watching a game show on television.

I can remember a lot of the conversations Flash and I had on the garage roof while the fertilizing machine grumbled up and down the rows of corn, swinging its headlight. We talked about Max and Jane constantly, and we couldn't praise them enough. I would list what I loved about Max: his name, his eyes, his voice. I liked how when we'd first danced and I'd stepped on his foot he hadn't minded, and I said to Flash that he was like that—that he, Flash, probably wouldn't have minded either if I'd stepped on his foot while we were dancing. I said I liked it when Max smiled because he smiled with his whole face.

None of this information could have been particularly enthralling, but it mattered to me, and I didn't usually tell my secrets. I felt like I could say anything to Flash. I'd never met another boy my age who I could talk to as easily as I talked to him. "How long have you liked Max?" he asked me once, and sheepishly I told him it had been almost a year, ever since the first night of dancing school. Max had asked me to be his partner that week, and two weeks later and once more in the spring, and in between I had seen him three or four times. I had even made a list of the times Max Huddle had spoken to me. I showed it to Flash, and he crumpled it up and lit it with one of his matches. "You don't know him very well," Flash pointed out. "Shannon, maybe you're just—"

"What?" I said, defensive already.

"Maybe you just like liking him."

"You're right," I replied. "It doesn't make sense." But I was lying. It made perfect sense.

The one thing I couldn't tell Flash, in spite of all our other confidences, was that Max Huddle had a father who drove a big, blue Mercedes which he kept in a section of their garage that was separately locked. Even Max's mom didn't have a key. Almost every Saturday morning, he would drive the blue Mercedes over to the country club skeet field where he would blast away at clay pigeons with a 12-gauge shotgun. Max often went with him.

However irrational he found me, Flash did try earnestly to find ways for me to get together with Max. "He's good at tennis, right?" Flash asked. I nodded. "Okay, so call him up and say let's play a game. Or a match. Or a chukker. Whatever the hell those are called. And then you're on the court . . ."

"I don't play tennis," I interrupted.

"What are you saying, Shannon? You're a prep. Of course you play tennis."

"I'm terrible at it."

"Okay." Flash paused. "Okay, you say I need help. I'm terrible at tennis."

"Flash, I'm not going to call him.

"You've danced with him, yeah?" I shook my head yes. "He knows who you are."

"But he'll think I'm weird."

"You are weird." Flash grinned at me. "You are the best weird girl I know."

"Thanks a lot," I said. "I'm not calling him. And I'm not weird."

"Then why would he think you are?"

"Oh, Flash, shut up." But I said it cheerfully, even affectionately. I liked Flash because he really listened.

Sometimes we'd compete to see who was more in love. He would start off, "I think Jane is the goddess of the sun." He'd go on about how her auburn, shimmering hair was like the sun, and then I'd say, "If Max was stranded in the desert, I would walk across a thousand miles of sand to take him a glass of water."

"It would evaporate," Flash pointed out, so I modified the plan. I would quench Max's thirst with my own saliva. Flash said he gave that one a nine, and I stood up on the roof and curtsied, delighted by my own ingenuity. If Becky or Jane had been there, they would have thought I was gross, and I'm sure someone like Kevin would have been equally as scornful of our childish game. But it was only Flash and me, and though I didn't realize it until later, I was very happy during those nights on the roof.

Secretly, I collected small pieces from the Witch's Cauldron, the store that Flash's mother ran. Earrings, roach clips, tarot cards, frangipani incense sticks, a baggie full of Moroccan trading beads. It wasn't the kind of stuff I needed my parents, or even Jane and Becky, to know about. Even Flash didn't know. I kept it all in the bottom drawer of my extra bureau, under the old doll's clothing. As a child, I believed that objects had mystical properties, properties that kept away wicked spirits. All the fairy tales that the grownups read to us back then insisted that we had to believe in evil beings, in witches and bad godmothers and giants and little green froglike men who swung from mushrooms on cobweb swings. You needed garlic nailed to your front door, you needed rabbits' feet and charms to carry in your pocket or to wear around your neck. Nobody ever found out about all the things I kept in my secret drawer. These things are probably still there. At least, I hope they're still there.

We were so innocent that summer we even invited Flash to the pool at our country club. We thought we were being daring. We could pretend we didn't know what we were doing, his being half black and the club never having had any non-white members. But what could they do? They wouldn't dare kick us out, or even say anything. It was exciting to imagine a scene. Flash with his baggy pants being confronted by a phalanx of men in tennis whites, or even Max's father with his 12-gauge shotgun.

Nothing happened, of course.

At least, nothing happened until we were walking out of the parking lot.

Flash suddenly said, "I guess you ladies think you're real warriors for social justice."

We were silent for almost a minute. Then Becky said, "What the hell are you talking about?"

"Oh, come on," Flash smirked at her. "You think I don't know about this club? A little tea for you, Virginia? Shall we take out the Mercedes or the Rolls?" His voice was high and phony.

"Flash, don't do this." Jane reached out to grasp one of his arms, but he pulled away from her, and that was how I knew he was really angry. He'd sometimes pretend to get irritated with Becky and me, sneering at us and making nasty comments, and then he'd turn around and say, "Just kidding," and we'd throw something at him. But he never joked like that with Jane, he was too much in love with her to joke, and so I knew he was serious. He was moving around so jerkily, twisting his head back and forth and thrusting out his arms, that he almost looked like he was dancing. "I still don't know what you're talking about," Becky said to him.

I wanted to tell her to shut up; she was about as bad at lying as I was. And I wanted to say to Flash that I was sorry for bringing him to the country club, but I didn't do anything. "How stupid do you think I am? Huh? I just want to know, do you feel sorry for me? Is that why? Pity?" He was pressing his lips together so hard that they were dark red, maroon even, and when he spoke, tiny bubbles of spit flew out. His usually slight lisp had become pronounced. "Huh? Pity or what?"

"Flash, stop it." Jane looked like she was going to cry.

"We were only swimming," Becky said. "Why does everything have to be such a big deal?" But Flash was already running out of the parking lot, away from the rows of shiny cars, and he left us there with dripping hair and bare feet that burned against the black pavement. We watched him go, and Becky said, as if to clarify things, "Oh, shit."

We didn't see him for a week. At night when the boyfriends came over to get Jane and Becky, I'd go to Jane's room and fall asleep. I missed Flash more than any of them. Then when he came back one evening, riding his bike, smiling goofily, I was so happy I ran off the porch to meet him. None of us ever apologized in words for what had happened at the country club, but Flash brought us presents, and so it happened like it always does that the wrong person had to say he was sorry. For Jane he had a serious-looking silver ring from his mother's shop. For Becky and me, elaborately wrapped packages with ribbons and bows that turned out to be cartons of cigarettes. "But I don't smoke," I reminded him.

"Then give them to me, damn it," Becky said. She reached for my carton.

"Maybe you should start." Flash wiggled his eyebrows at me. "Relax a little."

"No, thanks."

"Oh, Shannon, don't be pissed off at me." He crossed the porch and sat on my lap, and then he wrapped his arms around me, and I couldn't be annoyed because I was laughing. "Jesus Christ," he said. "You're too good of a girl." After that, Jane and Becky started talking at the same time, and it seemed stupid later, it seemed petty, to ask what he'd meant or whether it was a bad thing to be too good of a girl.

One afternoon, as I was heading home from the library, an old dark blue Toyota with white paint smeared across one fender pulled over and stopped. There was a squirrel's tail hanging from the antenna, and the radio was playing loud. I saw about six black faces looking at me, and I don't know which one said, "You seen Flash?" but I knew it was a female voice.

"No," I said stupidly. "Who?"

"Flash, starch face. You know the name."

"Of course I know the name."

"Of course you know the name," the voice came back imitating my whine.

I started walking a little faster but the car was gliding along right beside me.

"You tell Flash some of his friends be looking for him, you hear?"

"Yes," I said.

"Tell Flash some of his black friends be looking for him," whoever-she-was said. "Hear? You tell Flash that for us?"

"I hear," I said.

Then I got the nerve to stop and turn around and look at them. Somebody's older brother, I guess, was driving. He stared straight ahead.

"Why do you all want to know where he is?"

"Oh yawl. Why yawl want to know where he is, yawl." A few of them laughed uproariously.

"I meant all of you. Or any of you. I'd tell if I knew."

"You hiding him, yawl?" The voice was from the back seat.

I said, "He's always welcome in our neighborhood, thank you," but I doubted that I sounded very convincing or confident.

"Oh, I love your manners," the girl's voice again. "Tell him Jane called him. Sweet little Janie." The laughter again. You know Jane, don't you?"

Then the car started up fast and raced forward. I could see a trail of dust and hear the wheels squeal on the turn.

Later I asked Flash who they were. He said there were rumors going around among a group of girls that honkie women were going after their men. It had even gotten down to our age group. He started to laugh, as if flattered to be considered one of "their men," but he stopped when he saw my expression. He said it was no big deal.

What is there here that is not being told? I thought. I had a lot of experience with bragging boys telling stories, big dramatic stories, or exaggerated stories.

I imagined him again as a caped superhero, fighting intolerance. I felt better about inviting him to the country club. I imagined him inviting his friends, if they were his friends, those girls, to join us around the swimming pool the next time we went there.

That's how the story would end, I convinced myself. "Their men" and "our men" splashing each other in the face and throwing plastic toys while those girls from the car watched us and, sitting at the pool's edge with their legs slapping the water, tossed the toys back into the pool. No big deal.

Near the end of the summer, Flash began hanging out more with the skateboarders in Whistler Square and less with us. He'd still come by Jane's a couple of times a week, but Becky had broken up with her boyfriend by then, so there were three of us rather than just Flash and me goofing off on the roof. There was a particular night when all four of us sat on Jane's porch, getting drunk and reading *Changing Bodies, Changing Lives* and the story about the boy who got turned on by vacuum cleaners still seemed funny.

After her fourth beer, Becky stood up, flung out her arms extravagantly, and cried, "We love you, Flash. You're like our brother." She began kissing him, and as he was pulling her toward him, our eyes met. I got up and went inside. I could hear him say something to her out on the porch that sounded like, "Come on, Becky, not now."

I stood by the kitchen sink for awhile. I turned on the tap and watched the water swirl and gurgle down through the rubber flaps of the disposal. Sure we were just fooling around. We were kids. We were supposed to act like this. I could almost see Becky now, sitting on Flash's lap, making a face like she'd just swallowed something cool and sweet that left a pucker. I'd seen that expression from her before when she was around boys. Jane would be sitting cross-legged on the rattan sofa. Flash would smile directly at Becky, mostly for Jane's benefit, but Jane wouldn't care, she'd continue reading a magazine, pretending to ignore them. Flash would begin to gesture, an arm flung out this way, then that, as if getting ready for a huge embrace.

No, that's impossible. He would be looking at Jane directly to see how she reacted.

"What's with Shannon?" somebody would say.

"She's uncool, that's all. She misses a lot."

Jane would light a cigarette. "How about the two of you up on the garage roof all summer, Flash?"

Would Flash say anything, or would he just smirk?

Jane would shake out her match. "Does she still have a thing for that pathetic Max Huddle?"

Becky would say, "The guy whose dad drives around in that big blue Mercedes and shoots at fake birds every Saturday?"

Flash would only laugh and say, "God, I feel wasted. How about another beer?"

And standing by the sink, I suddenly thought, "So this is how it is."

A car would pull up suddenly, catching the porch in its headlights, Jane's father would step out briskly and come around to the porch door. He would knock softly. "What are you people doing? Hey you kids, it's time to go home."

Now Flash stood beside me at the sink. "A little uptight this evening, my dear? You left the room, Jane left to go for a walk. Does our behavior disgust you?" He was teasing, of course, but he was right.

I shut my eyes for a second, as if things would be different when I opened them. Nothing was different.

"You've been fooling around with Becky since the start of the summer, haven't you?" I said.

"No, dear."

"Even Jane, between boyfriends, has been going up to the attic with you."

"No, dear."

He was lying. I could tell by the sarcasm. And it was my own blindness that made me sad, not their behavior.

The telephone rang, and I reached across the counter. A voice said, "Uh, hi . . . My name's Cherish and a friend gave me your number. She said maybe I could crash at your place if I needed to?"

I glanced over at Flash. His face was blank, distressed, or was I imagining this?

"Who's the friend?" I asked into the phone. "Who's that, the friend, I mean?"

"Her name is Star Bluebird? We met out at Mendocino? Last year?"

"She's a friend of Jane's?" Flash was blinking his eyes, raising his eyebrows up and down. Trying to clown.

"This is Jane's house. Do you want Jane? She's gone out for a walk, I think."

Flash nodded. He gave two thumbs up.

"Who's Jane?" the voice on the telephone said.

"What number . . ." I began.

Then I tried to look for Jane's number on the telephone, then I remembered it, but the voice went on, "Who's Jane?"

"What number . . ." I said again. Flash was clasping his hands like a mime, praying. I thought for a moment, then I said, "Oh sure, Star Bluebird. Far-out chick. Well, no biggy. Where are you now?"

"At my grandparents' place. But I can't stay. They're kicking me out again."

"Well, Cherish," I said, "people drift in and out of this pad. It's definitely a crazy scene, but if you like craziness, no problem. We've moved though. We're at sixty-nine Cedar Street. You got that? Sixty-nine Cedar?"

"Whoa. Let me get a pencil or something."

I hung up and followed Flash back onto the porch. Becky's head was down. Then she looked up. "Jane was angry. She went out for a walk."

We sat there in the dark for awhile listening to music. I knew Becky felt bad, but as usual, I couldn't think of anything to say that would make us all feel better.

At the sound of the first cries, we sat forward, giving each other did-you-hear-what-I-heard looks. Then we heard another scream and then another, and by then we were on our feet. Flash had trouble tying his sneakers, and I ran ahead. Pretty soon we were all stumbling through the bushes at the edge of the cornfield, in the light of the moon, toward the direction of Jane's screams. We could hear them over the moan of the fertilizing machine.

Five or six black girls were running from the scene, caught briefly in the headlight. They must have been posted outside the house, perhaps many nights in a row, waiting for the moment.

They had shaved off all of Jane's hair.

She was sitting there holding her head, crying like a baby. I began to cry too, remembering all the times Flash had praised her hair.

Flash sat on the ground between us and reached out his arms for all of us. He held us as if we were little kids.

When Jane's parents arrived later, they told us to go on home. They said they could take care of it.

Five years from now, will I still think about the cornfield behind Jane's porch, or the motorcycles that beeped as they passed, or even Flash's flaring matches? Will I care about the skateboarders behind Whistler Square, or that book, *Changing Bodies, Changing Lives*? We will all have changed. Just yesterday, my mother came into my room and sat down on the bed with a pile of brochures in her hand. "Well, dear," she said, "it's about time to start thinking about college. And good news! We've contacted Grosvenor Associates in Boston, and Jane Grosvenor herself will take you under her wing for the next two years. She'll work with you personally, advise you on your course selections and advanced placements through sophomore and junior years, and I hear they practically write the college application essays for you. Not that you necessarily need that kind of help, but I'm sure you'll benefit from her advice. She's really such a sweet person and you are so lucky."

Five years from now, will Flash be in college? Where will he go?

We didn't see Flash after the summer was over. He disappeared from our lives the same way he'd appeared. Jane wore a wig for awhile, but her hair grew in nicely and nobody ever knew for sure who'd done it. We went to a different school than he did, and we were busy with homework and soccer and boyfriends: Becky had found a new one, and I still mooned over Max Huddle. Becky was the first person in the ninth grade, the only person at Davis Middle School, to get a license, and sometimes when we drove through Whistler Square we'd see Flash in the parking lot of the Snackmart. The skaters were skinny and dirty looking, and they dressed in black. When they weren't flying through the air on their skateboards, they sat on the curb and smoked. They were like a family, all those shaggy-haired boys, and at first it was difficult for me to picture Flash skating with them, gentle, joking Flash, but pretty soon what was difficult was remembering how he'd spent so much time with three silly girls like us.

What girls said about skaters was that they were better to fool around with. The palms of their hands were thick and red from scrapes, and they might not look like much, but it didn't matter when you felt those palms across your breasts or around you. By then I didn't dare, but I wanted badly to ask Jane and Becky if it was true, if that was how it had been with Flash.

The next time we saw him was during the winter. He showed up at a dance at our school, arriving in a pack of other skaters. They'd increased security at the school. I felt ashamed wondering how he and his friends had managed to crash the party. The dance was one of those horrible middle school deals, where streamers blind you at every turn and depressed girls weep in front of the bathroom mirror. Halfway through, when I was standing near the stairwell that connected the gym and the cafeteria, Flash approached. "Want to dance?" he asked. The music was so loud I could hardly understand him.

"No," I said.

"Huh?" He leaned forward, so I was speaking directly into his ear.

"Yes," I said.

"Huh?"

"Not to this song." That was what he finally heard. He shrugged and walked away, and he never spoke to me again directly.

I nearly went after him, and later I wished I had, but my reflexes had always been a little slow around Flash. After a couple of hours, when Becky and I were leaving, we passed him on the same stairwell. My eyes met his, and I couldn't look away even as I climbed the cement steps. There were a couple of skaters lounging there, scowling and sticking out their huge feet so we had to climb over them. The skaters had become popular with the girls at our school, and one of them, the guy who spoke, had some eighth grader in a green skirt nestled between his legs. "What's going on with you and her?" he asked Flash, gesturing at me. He was smoking a cigarette, and when he moved his arm, he dropped ashes on the eighth grader.

Flash and I were still watching each other when he said, "I'm in love with her, but she won't talk to me."

I was stunned. I wanted to tell him it wasn't like that, that he was being goofy again, of course I would talk to him, but I remained silent because I could not believe I'd heard him correctly, and if I had, I didn't know if I was elated or horrified. He liked Jane, he always had, and that meant he couldn't be in love with me. And I wanted to say that to him but not with the skaters listening, and already too much time had gone by and I knew that anything I said would come out sounding awkward, stupid. "Hurry up." Becky grabbed my arm. "Are you coming or what?" She continued up the steps, and I followed, stupidly.

"He says he loves you," the skater called. "You're just gonna leave?"

I said, "No," but my voice was so quiet that none of them heard me. When I paused at the top of the stairs I wasn't surprised to hear the skater say, "What a bitch. She couldn't be worth it, man." I wished I could make myself turn back, but Becky kept tugging my arm, digging her fingernails into me. "Come on, Shannon," she whispered, but I'm sure her voice carried. "Let's go," she said.

She said, "It's only Flash."

At The Aquarium

Names from the past float by.
They are like white fish in a white tank,
Then black fish in a black tank.
Every so often you hear the slosh.
Into your ear comes a name. "That was Williams," you say.
A sharp image appears in your head.
You shake your head.
Maybe you see a smile different
from the others.
A twisted leer of shark teeth. Williams.
The names from the past float by
Like fish in a quiet sea.

Each Petal Is Perfect

This may be the bed
you slept in,
but do not rest there now,
tiny memory.
Do not lie down
in the whitening shade
of our garden,
light-aired ghost. Go somewhere else
and sleep among the winter flowers
and the dim lanterns.

As I stood at the window tonight
your strange petals looked in, saying,
"Each blossom is perfect
enclosing itself in a winter flower,
making pain."

Overcoats

"Aren't you taking a little more than you really need?" Baxter's wife said. She stared into the car, shielding her eyes, while Baxter brushed snow off the rear window with his mitten. Inside the car two pairs of skis lay across the seat backs—the downhills and the cross-countries—with the appropriate poles. The boots that went with each pair lay on the backseat next to the rubber galoshes, a set of L.L. Bean lace-ups, and assorted gym shoes. Also in the back seat was a huge duffel bag stuffed with winter clothes, a pile of blankets, and two shopping bags filled with books. Some of the books had already spilled onto the floor of the car.

"Two weeks," he said. "You can get a lot done in two weeks." He pointed his mitten at her. "You always take books along when we go on weekends and never read them. I am going to read these babies. Every one of them. I am going to read them down to the last page. Maybe get in some skiing, too. For mental health."

Baxter's eight-year-old son hunched up his shoulders and slapped his gloves together in the cold. He was wearing a new jacket, of which we will be hearing more later, and he said, "Will you write, Dad?"

"Will I write?" Baxter's voice expressed mock outrage. "What else would I be doing at a writers' conference in Vermont?"

It was January, the spiritless winter, full of short days and shorter tempers, but Baxter felt lighthearted and adventurous. The family was clear financially, he had managed to draw down some advance vacation time, and so he had filled out an application and submitted it to the writers' conference along with a poem and a check. The check had taken as long to write, caused him almost as much anguish as the poem; but when he received a letter stating that "The Faculty Committee feels you might make good use of the program," he decided to go, ignoring the letter's obvious ambiguities.

"You'll be gone how long?" his wife had asked.

"Two weeks."

"Two weeks." She sat at the kitchen table eating a carrot. "They're going to teach you how to write poetry in two weeks?"

"Not teach," Baxter said. "They can't teach poetry. They can't really teach you anything. What I need is something like a community, a sense of—this is hard to explain—a sense of audience to visualize, an audience that I can imagine when I write a poem, so I won't feel so alone and futile. That's it. I need to make myself able to imagine an audience." It was, as he had said, hard to explain.

"Why don't you try to imagine us?" his wife said. "Home alone, two little children without their father and all the hassles with the children's carpool while I'm at work. What do I tell the Harrisons about the carpool?"

"Oh God," Baxter said. "Don't tell the Harrisons where I'm going. They'll think I've been defeated by the rat race. Just tell them something they can understand. Tell them I left you."

* * *

When Baxter awoke the second morning of the conference, he got up and stood for a long time before the window.

He was so accustomed to the noise and congestion of the city that the beauty of the winter morning seemed savage and foreign. Vermont's distant hills and studded conifers suggested a Siberian setting, and the strong sun, pouring its light into the quadrangle, struck the brick buildings of the campus with an intensity as commanding as a searchlight.

For a time, Baxter played with the Siberian analogy in his mind. It was not entirely satisfactory. In the Siberia that he imagined, the residents were subject to occasional acts of mercy from the regime in power or from its successors. Party lines could be revised, the inhabitants could be set free, entire nations could be liberated.

But this particular gulag, this writers' workshop he was attending, contained people of a different sort. Far from family, friends, and loved ones, with only peripheral access to newspapers, television, and basic sanitation, they were beholden to a cruel and lying regime from which there could be no escape. They were prisoners of the imagination, trapped in—Baxter's mind groped for a metaphor, "the eternal archipelago of literature"—and promptly rejected it.

Many events of the previous day—registration day—contributed to his sense of abandonment and gathering fear. The brittle hairstyles of the women at breakfast, hair partially dried and then frozen in the morning walk across campus, seemed to reflect the mass regimentation of a malevolent hairdresser. During the orientation sessions, the speaker prefaced his remarks by announcing that a lost earring had been discovered in the snow. He held up before the audience an object so large and extravagant in design that the ear seemed to be still attached.

That evening, as Baxter took a shower, he tried to think of a poem. All he could think of was decorum. How would he be perceived here? Frivolous probably. Any exact account of his immaturity would reveal memories and thoughts of people he had loved, but they would be attached mostly to surface detail, places where he had loved them—beaches, waiting rooms, airports. Was this enough for poetry? Could decorum be transformed into a mode of speech? Probably not.

He stepped from the shower and was beginning to towel off when a woman in a dirty uniform burst into the lavatory, almost tripping over her mop and clanking pail. As Baxter brushed his teeth, she maneuvered the mop around his toes in such a vigorous manner that he felt the need to reassure her.

"Thanks," he said. "You're doing great work."

"Oh," she replied, "thank you. We're not the normal person who does the bathrooms." Her expressions revealed deranged lines accenting the eyes.

The wind moaned around the windows as she continued her mopping, as if nature itself required him to say something more. But he wasn't so crazy that he didn't know how uninteresting his anxiety would be to most people, the banality of evil being far exceeded by the banality of neurosis.

"How long are we going to allow ourselves to be treated like this?" the woman demanded. The radiator clanked and sputtered.

"It's not the money," she continued angrily, "it's the way we are treated. We told the program director he was kidding himself about his reasons for wanting to expand the visiting writers program. He thought he was being altruistic, and we thought it had more to do with wanting big names. We've published a bit in our day," she grumbled. "But no, it will never do even to allude to our problems as visiting writers. And obviously, you don't care about that. So all right, all right." She replaced the mop in the bucket with a gesture of sarcastic deference. The upper body inclination made her seem shorter than she really was.

"I'm sorry to hear this," Baxter said. "It must be excruciating for you."

"Nor do we need your sympathy, sir, or your condescension to the tedium of the poet's life."

The next day, in an effort to allay his anxiety after a blizzard of seminars, workshops, and lectures, he decided to try some exercise. Late that afternoon he appeared at the gym, self-consciously attired in a sweatsuit. He joined in with the basketball players. Some of them moved adroitly, the gestures timed and well-practiced, but there were enough like himself, flinging the ball up randomly and missing by wide margins, that he began to feel almost easy, almost triumphant.

After awhile he noticed a young man who was aiming at the backboard quite slowly and deliberately. He would take his time, set his feet, look up toward the basket, bounce the ball once or twice, then set himself again. He was sinking the 15-footers with astonishing regularity because, unless Baxter was mistaken, he was the same young man, a poet, that Baxter had observed walking slowly across the campus with a white cane, often with someone at his side.

Baxter watched as the poet flexed his legs and hurled the ball upward. The shot missed, and the ball rebounded directly into Baxter's hands. The poet seemed to know where the ball was.

"Could you bounce it over?" he asked. "If you pass it with a bounce, I can hear it."

The poet took aim. Once again he missed but not by much. Baxter hurried after the ball, then strolled up and handed it to him.

"How do you do that?" Baxter asked. It immediately occurred to him that the question was impulsive and rather tactless. He thought it might be acceptable in the casual atmosphere of a gym and in light of his guileless curiosity. Also, the poet himself had brought up the subject.

"I can hear it," the poet said.

"Hear it?"

"Sure."

He set himself and took aim, pausing long enough to let Baxter ask him, "How can you hear it?"

"I just hear it."

He bounced the ball on the floor and caught it with both hands.

"You can hear the rim of a basketball hoop? When you aim at it?"

The poet smiled. Then, he started to laugh. "I'm putting you on. But I can sure hear the swish when the ball goes through."

He let fly.

Swish.

They took a few more shots, introduced themselves, then headed outside. Baxter held the poet's coat for him at the door, noticing how it resembled his own, but looked at least ten years older. He, himself, must be ten years older than the poet, he thought.

The afternoon gloom had lowered. The wind was coming from behind them, at the same speed they were walking, and the snow was flaky and slow, its movement more horizontal than vertical. They seemed to be moving without moving, following a course that took them in a circle. Paths that had been shoveled were already covered by snow, and the poet's white cane made cautious forward arcs. He had declined Baxter's arm when it was offered.

The poet's story began when he was about the same age as Baxter's own son, eight years old. He had begun to feel sick much of the time, with dizziness and vomiting. His nausea was interpreted, by his angry and divorcing parents, as a reaction to their marital troubles. The child psychologist to whom he was sent was unable to diagnose the brain tumor immediately, and the delay led to the need for drastic surgery. He still retained, he told Baxter, partial vision in one eye.

They were now walking slowly along a path that led from the gym to the dormitories. The walkway seemed more treacherous now. The banks stood two or three feet high on either side.

"Please be careful," Baxter said. "These paths are dangerous."

"I'll be okay. Is this my dormitory? If it is, I'll leave you here and go back to the Braille. I do my first drafts on a Braille typewriter. I need the feel of the poem on my fingers."

"How do you find the time to write up here? All the workshops, seminars, readings?"

"You make the time," he said. "You have to be determined. Enjoyed talking to you."

Baxter felt the same way about talking to him, but it was difficult to imagine the source of the poet's enjoyment. All they had discussed, as far as Baxter could recollect, was the poet's blindness and his childhood pain.

As the days continued the campus and its surroundings began to feel more comfortable. There was no party line of the imagination after all, and in the cafeteria people would talk about their work in a subdued way, banter about their homes and families while exchanging wallet-sized photographs. One man was obsessed with real estate.

"I just can't get the listings," he would complain. "It's not the selling. That's the easy part. It's getting the listings. You have to know important people who like you and want to help you. You can't be off in some…" He laughed uneasily and looked around him. "…other world. It's all hustle, like getting published."

At last, the final evening arrived with its brief ceremony. Baxter sat in the last row of chairs, near the back of the darkened reading room, a few spaces from where a small child was seated in her mother's lap. As the speakers read their works, he found himself playing a surreptitious game of monkey see, monkey do with the two-year-old. The child's efforts to distract him, to keep him from becoming restless and squirmy during the ceremony, were not entirely successful, because Baxter had lost his overcoat. He was furious, and he wanted it back.

He had looked for it earlier on the coatrack outside the reading room, where he thought he had left it. Now, with the ceremony concluded, the lights on, and people gathering in small groups, he began his search more purposefully.

Trying to retrace his steps from earlier in the evening, he returned to the main hall where the graduation dinner had taken place. It was not in the small cloakroom off the dining hall, nor had he any reason to believe it would be there. He had a clear memory of removing it from that place, shrugging it over his shoulders, and walking across the campus to the reading room. He was certain that he had hung it on the long row of hangers in the hallway outside that room, somewhere in the middle of the rack. But it wasn't there.

His exasperation grew toward a self-protective rage that tried to masquerade as tough-mindedness. As he moved back and forth between the hallway and the reading room, looking under chairs and tables, examining every coat that resembled his own, people began to notice his agitation.

"Hey, that's mine," someone said as Baxter examined a coat on a chair. "It was mine the last time you looked at it too."

He threw out his hands foolishly. "I'm sorry. It's just becoming an obsession."

One young woman smiled in a kindly way as he slumped down next to her on a stuffed sofa. "I blame myself for everything, too," she said. "Don't worry. It'll show up."

"Except," Baxter said sourly, "by tomorrow everybody will be gone."

Somebody leaned across her, looked at Baxter intensely, and said, "Have you ever read *The Overcoat*, by Gogol?"

Baxter hadn't.

"It's a sad, sad story. It's the saddest story ever told."

Another person turned away from a small group of people and said, over his shoulder, "You know, that's interesting. I read somewhere that only we, here, in the twentieth century, find the story sad. Those nineteenth-century Russians took the guy to be something of a jerk. They laughed at him."

"It's still the saddest story ever told," insisted the first.

"Jerk," said the other. "A sad jerk."

Baxter had no taste for this. Excusing himself, he continued the search, but when he finally went to bed, after once again retracing his steps across the campus to the dining hall, he was still without his overcoat.

As he lay on the bed, fully clothed but with the lights out, a memory began to shape itself. It was the memory of an afternoon approximately two months before, a pleasant autumn afternoon, a Saturday. He was with his children on a museum excursion in the City. Sleep would not come for him as his memory rotated with the cycle of the incident that involved—once again—a lost outer garment. A jacket belonging to his eight-year-old son.

His three-year-old daughter was also present at the McDonald's. As she dipped Baxter's tea bag into her orange drink, she was saying, "I love everybody." She continued in a singsongy tone, seemingly mesmerized by the bobbing tea bag, and addressing no one in particular. "I love everyone in my family. I love my Dad. I love my Mom. I love my brother. I love myself. I love my cat. I love my house. I love everything."

"Do you even love your stuffed frog?" her brother asked.

She looked at him, puzzled. "I don't have a stuffed frog, Nicholas."

Her elbow nudged some broken cookies off the table. They landed in Baxter's lap. He asked Julia if she would allow Nicholas to read to them from the Happy Meal box.

"I'll only let him read it…if he invites me…to his next birthday party."

"Okay," Nicholas said. "You can come." Julia handed him the container with its cartoon figures, puzzles, mazes, and bright aphorisms. He studied it. Baxter popped one of the cookies into his mouth.

"Those are mine," the children complained in unison.

"Then what are they doing in my lap? "Baxter said.

"Dad, Dad," said Nicholas. "You're supposed to be on a diet."

ALL RISE

"These are on my diet. Doctor Baxter's Junk Food Diet. Six Happy Meals a day, ten glasses of water, and all the cookies you can eat. These are high in—what's it called?—fiber? Try one." They began to discuss their weights. Baxter reminded Nicholas of a time when it seemed he would weigh 30 pounds for the rest of his life. Then, suddenly, it was 40, then 45, then 60.

"How much does Julia weigh?" Nicholas asked. Baxter could not remember, so he questioned her. Julia smiled pleasantly and held up both fists, gradually extending her fingers one by one in an inquiring way.

"That's ten, Julia," Nicholas said. "Even Smokey the cat weighs more than that."

Julia looked thoughtful, then blurted out, "Ninety-ten pounds?"

"Maybe she's been lifting weights," Nicholas said, enjoying her. "Hey, Dad, Dad. Can you tell us the story about the little, green man?"

Later on they discovered the loss of the jacket. Could they have left it at the McDonald's? They retraced their steps. It was mid-afternoon, balmy, with no wind. Baxter stormed through "Don't Walk" lights at intersections, a child in each hand. The manager at the McDonald's had no jacket in his lost and found. Back at the museum, Baxter questioned corridor guards, ticket-takers, uniformed officials with walkie-talkies, ladies in smocks selling postcards. No one had seen it, no one had found it, no one had turned it in.

Its cost rested heavy on Baxter's mind. It had been purchased two days before, to replace a jacket that Nicholas had lost two days before that. Baxter was not being kind about it, for it seemed that each time he delivered himself a barrage of stern, parental commentary, Nicholas would turn lighthearted within a few moments, as if forgetting what he had forgotten. In a cadenced voice Baxter reminded Nicholas of his obligations, now that he was eight years old, to keep track of his own things. Baxter enumerated the many services that Nicholas' parents had provided for him in his infancy that should now no longer be necessary. Baxter spoke of future parental services, as well as individual privileges, that could hardly be bestowed on an eight-year-old so scatterbrained.

A wisecrack lingered in Baxter's memory—a limpid, pointless joke that had shot out of his mouth as the three of them stood in the museum, toward closing time, facing a skeleton model of a tyrannosaurus rex. The remark somehow linked the enormity of his son's offense with the scale of the prehistoric animal, the size of the jacket such an animal might have worn in those Cretaceous times, the likelihood of its being lost. Whether ruefully humorous or not, the comment's effect on Baxter's son was devastating.

"All right!" Nicholas cried out at last, clenching his fists. Then, he sat down on the short, stone barrier that separated them from the display, and, with his head in his hands, the tears came. They would not stop—nothing could stop his crying, not even his sister, who had previously seemed to be slightly enjoying his discomfiture. Now, she approached Nicholas tenderly, sat down next to him, and touched his forearm. She looked back at Baxter with dark and serious eyes.

Because Nicholas was Baxter's firstborn, Baxter was not fully aware that an eight-year-old and a jacket are mutually inhospitable, especially in early autumn, when the weather might call for a jacket in the morning and a light cotton shirt in the afternoon. This particular afternoon, the third-grader's thoughts might even have been concentrated on an opportunity for a wandering and dreamy afternoon of intimacy with his father and sister, in an undisciplined world of food in astonishingly garish boxes, long stories on park benches about little, green men, and the random wonderment of a museum. Such an afternoon had now been ruined. But it was not the absent jacket that had ruined it.

As Baxter played the memory, trying to retract the impulsive comment, or at least to rephrase it less hurtfully, he became increasingly troubled and sleepless. His memory revolved with this incident, and the incident refused to change. It refused to transform itself into anything other than a small vision of the world's injustices and his own complicity in them. His son was both his past and his future, and it seemed as if they had been cast out on a very precarious limb together. Baxter could not fall asleep.

He decided to make one last search for the missing overcoat.

The lights were still blazing in the deserted reading room where the graduation had taken place. On a table by the wall, a bowl of hardening cheese dip, with a lopsided floret of broccoli stuck in it, rested beside a jug of white wine in a plastic tub of melted ice. Baxter looked under the table, then circled the room, eyeing the chairs.

In the outside hallway he saw an overcoat. It was in the exact location where he remembered leaving his own, now conspicuous in the long line of empty wire hangers. It hung in the middle of the rack, a similar color, but a shabbier version of his own overcoat. Everyone had left the party, one overcoat had remained. Baxter seized it with the same violence he now felt toward its careless and probably wine-woozy owner. First, he all but strangled the coat for causing him such a night of deep disquietude. Then, as he wrestled it off the hanger to make off with it, ransom it perhaps, a piece of paper fluttered to the floor. Baxter searched the coat's pockets for evidence of ownership. There was none. He bent down to pick up the paper, but it was blank on both sides. Baxter started to crumple it, then decided to return it to the coat's pocket. The blank piece of paper seemed strange. It was thick and rough-textured. Holding it closer to his eyes, he noticed tiny marks and indentations, but his eyes told him less than the feel of it on his fingers.

He returned the slip of paper, with its Braille markings, into the pocket and put the jacket back on the hanger. A sad jerk! That's what he was! For the second time that evening, rage was transformed to distress. But this time, when the sadness came, it was of a different quality—a strange, deep, calming kind of sadness that made sleep possible and welcome. Somewhere, miles away, his son lay asleep, dreaming, perhaps, of prehistoric animals and journeys of discovery. It seemed they could be capable of great intimacy now.

The next morning Baxter made one final inspection. On the hallway coatrack, the blind poet's overcoat, which he had wanted to steal the night before, was missing. In its place, on exactly the same hanger, was Baxter's. It seemed like a merciful intercession. As he stood there he tried to imagine the words he would choose to tell his son the overcoat story. The words might contain an apology, he hoped. He thought, "This is my son," and he thought, "this is my life." His son was eight years old and waiting for all the stories his father might try to tell him.

Shrine

We were going to Boyne to ski? Got lost around Indian River? There's snow thickening on the road. Robbie says, "We're not going to make it up there tonight." He's tired from all the beers, plus we've been passing a little ganja around the car, the four of us. The smoke's quite thick and the car reeks.

Then, through the windshield, the headlights pick up this sign for the world's biggest crucifix. "Shit! Let's check that sucker out," Robbie says.

We follow the sign? We get to the parking lot and circle around? You can barely see the thing—just a big shaft sticking up through the snow and darkness. You can see some feet on the bottom, though.

That's when Robbie dares me to climb it. There's this maintenance ladder that goes up it. With little rungs where you can stick your feet and hold on.

I go, "No way. No way I'm getting up that thing."

But here I am, right at the top of the world's biggest crucifix. I can almost see the face, but it's dark and snowy. The thing is made of some kind of metal, bronze maybe. Shit, not the first time I've done something stupid for Robbie.

I yell down, "Hey, there's somebody already up here." Robbie and Max, I can hear them laughing way down below, laughing through the wind. Charlotte probably stayed in the car, the little pussy. Even though Charlotte's sort of a bitch, still, she can be pretty funny. She says all the guys that like me are total jerks. That I'm like a magnet for them because I like to do crazy stuff.

It's way cold up here. I'm not dressed warmly. Everything seems frozen. My nostrils are doing that thing where they stick together. Where they squinch up. My boots totally suck and I'm freezing my little butt off.

I can almost see the Jesus face now. It's metallic and icy and the eyes are way blank, except when snow hisses across the metal, and it almost changes the expression. It totally creeps me out.

It looks like Robbie at his creepiest. Me and Robbie have our creepy little dramas, too. Pretty gloomy, I guess. Sometimes he scares me, sometimes I feel like throwing up practically, or sometimes I'm just—I don't know... scared? I, like, don't know what to say. He has a bad temper. Ohmigod, he goes, like, totally mental sometimes. Or else he'll just hit me. Charlotte says, "Bad temper? Read my lips: how about asshole?" And she says the asshole thing long and loud for effect. And to think I had my tits done for him. Had my lips collagenized. Now my lips are fake, my hair color's fake, and lots of my body parts are fake, and Robbie says a lobotomy would've done me more good.

I look down through a swirl of snow and—ohmigod—a cop car. I can see the flasher turning slowly, sweeping the snowy lot and making everything look blue. Robbie and Max are trying to hide the beer cans, but the inside of the car must reek of weed, plus they left all that shit in plain sight.

A cop gets out and he's talking to them. Another one is looking through the car. After a while they're all—even Charlotte—shoved into the backseat. The cop car drives off.

Thanks, everybody! What am I doing? It's not like I even know. It's like I know where I am, but it's totally crazy because I feel like I totally don't. Like I'm here but I'm not here. That sounds so stupid, right? So totally dumb? Everybody forgot I was up here. That's how much they care. Leave me hanging up here on a ladder. And the wind blowing snow down the back of my neck and this creepy statue—this face.

Could I leer back at him? Could I make like a teenage vampire and drink his blood? My curved fangs would make a wet, slick sound as they slid down from my gums. I'd work my tongue over the fangs, then I'd push out my bristled tongue and begin to lick the statue's neck, my rough tongue scraping over the smooth, bronze throat. I tell the statue, "I'm so hungry, I need to feed."

Finally, I pretend it's real. I go like, "Now that we're alone, can I tell you some stuff?"

It stares back.

"First of all, I'm preggers. That's right. I think it was Robbie, but it could've been Max. How do you like that?"

No answer—the world's biggest crucifix has nothing to say.

"Next question. How come you get credit for all the good stuff that goes on, people giving thanks and all, but when things start to go bad, it's our sinful nature. That gets you off the hook; am I right?"

The world's biggest crucifix looks back at me blankly, the snow brushing its cheeks.

I'm like, "Shouldn't you stand up like a man and take the blame for some of the shit? Not just me being preggers, but earthquakes and floods and starving Africans?"

I'm starting to scare myself really good. Maybe I'll be left up here forever.

The snowflakes of the night continue to fall. I can't go down the ladder backward. I'm numb with terror. Maybe I'll see another cop car down in the parking lot to rescue me. Sometime—when? But going down is scarier than coming up.

Anyway, I'm stuck here. Whatever you say, here's a guy who doesn't go totally mental or hit you. He has no middle finger. Maybe he'll shake off the questions I asked him by claiming he doesn't exist, but that's a pretty lame excuse, a cop out, a typical guy thing; I can see right through it.

Now, all of a sudden I'm starting to feel nice—in a dizzy way. Ohmigod! What am I saying? This is like, what? I'm such a freak! Am I? Why am I telling you all this, like blabbing my head off? Right? Ohmigod! But I think about it. I try to think about stuff. I try to think about me as a person, like me skimming over the world. And how am I doing? I'm hanging from a ladder on the world's biggest crucifix. Days could pass and weeks and maybe years. What more could a girl possibly want?

Accomplice

Like many honest people, I dream constantly of committing a crime. I began by exploring the subject on the internet, Googling casually through the many selections: abuse --- domestic, sexual; arson --- gasoline, kerosene; bank robbery --- individual, gang induced; genocide --- racial, religious; graffiti; red light running; receiving stolen goods; shoplifting… these and all the others seemed to require either a taste for violence, or numerous accomplices.

To manage accomplices in most criminal undertakings, one has to be a "People Person," which I am not.

For awhile I was reduced to fantasy—murdering some helpless old pawn-broker, for example, with an axe, in order to prove my god-like qualities by the biblical enormity of the act. But what would such pretentiousness accomplish? A third-rate Russian novel, perhaps? A television series?

Here's Patricia Keenan with her tray, joining me for cafeteria lunch, as she often does. Patricia is our Chief Financial Officer, thought of as a "comer" on the street. She receives a very slim daily financial summary compared to those used by her male colleagues and subordinates. She relies more on data from her many trading floor contacts, many of whom she has reportedly enticed with promises of "favors". She's the best-accessorized CFO on Wall Street. Bergdorf Goodman sends her racks of clothing every week. She also has a grievously unsatisfactory marriage.

Our relationship is unambiguous. She wants something. What she wants is unclear at present.

"Sit down, Patricia," I say. "Do join me so we can continue our conversation."

"Please don't stand when I come to the table, Harold. It is manly, gallant and horribly sexist."

I should mention that Patricia and I both work for Falstaff Capitol, not the biggest hedge fund on the street, but one of the most audacious.

Patricia raises her soupspoon, blows on it gently. "Still having criminal fantasies?" she asks. "Our Google monitors are quite interested in your research."

"I'm not trying to cover my tracks," I respond. "I'm hoping those monitor-guys will pick up information I might be missing. When they confront me with it I'll be able to expand my efforts with the information I receive from their questions."

"You know the mistake most of them make?" Patricia shoves her soup bowl aside and leans forward. She whispers scornfully, "All the pension fund managers? All the hedge fund geniuses? All the pentagon contract riggers? They stupidly buy big SUV's. They renovate their houses. They vacation in the Alps. They send their kids to Andover."

"No self discipline."

"About that idea you were quote-unquote researching the other day?" She gives me a sideways look. "Are you serious or just playing around?"

"Speaking off the monitor," I said, "I can't do it. I'm not going to take an axe to your husband."

"Not that. The other idea." She's blinking rapidly. "How could we pull it off, technically speaking?"

"First we contact the state's business licensing department and get a license to do business as some entity with Falstaffian words like "fall" and "staff" or some other variation on our company name. "Folly Staff," "Full Stash." Anything that looks reasonable as a check endorsement by financial people. The first customer makes a deposit of, say, $15,000 to his regular account at Falstaff. You guarantee it in our own account "doing business as Folly and Staff." The second customer makes an investment of $30,000—half of which we credit to the first customer's account and so on."

"I see," her elbows are on the table, her chin in her knuckles. "The process continues as the sums in the 'Folly Staff' account get larger and larger."

"Basically it's what the Enron folks and their successors --- our current 'analysts' --- have been trying to accomplish." Except those particular embezzlers forgot to take off for Venezuela or wherever at the right time. That's the hardest part," I tell her. "Knowing when to stop, knowing when to disappear."

"My husband should disappear. He doesn't know I'm having an affair," she announces suddenly. She winks at me. She does not use the past tense. She does not seem to have thought before she spoke. In her greed and lust, she seems to have ignored the fact that we are not having an affair. But she has spoken the words, she has transformed herself into a married woman who is having an affair would like me to murder her husband. Should I sympathize, ignore the comment? Is it even for my benefit?

"I'd leave your husband out of it," I finally say. "Listen, let me tell you about phase two."

While she looks at me intently, her eyes a bit moist, I describe our new product.

"Product!" she says suddenly. "In America you don't need product; all you need is cash flow."

"There are," I begin, "60,000 business travelers in America today, and they have all sorts of needs --- planning and booking, en route services, post-travel reporting, unused ticket redemption. We'll deliver—under the name of Fully-Staffed Travel—all these services to travel marketers. We'll offer credit and identity-theft protection to their customers. As soon as we have acquired the personal information needed to protect their identities, we securitize their identities and sell them in large batches, represented by commercial paper, to banks and brokerage houses. In the event of defaults on individual credit card accounts, the investors who bought Identity Bonds will absorb the losses rather than the credit card companies. When the debt gets large enough, a few brokerage houses fail, the federal government moves in and bails everybody out, and happiness reigns in the land."

"Where do we go? Where do we go after we've stolen every identity in America and made it worthless?"

For a moment we are silent. At the end of the cafeteria the TV screen is showing the stock market reports, then the sports scores, then the weather. The numbers flash and jiggle indiscriminately, and arrows drop up, down, and sideways.

"I was thinking Hiva Oa," I said. "It's not as well known as Ua Pou, but it has larger palms, clearer waters, and more anonymity." My mind is now wheeling with potential mishaps and dangers. Is it possible that the second part of the scheme is too grandiose? Who really wants to live in a hut on Hiva Oa?

"Congratulations," Patricia says. "You're lucky. When it comes to lovers, my choices range from impulsive to irresponsible. Hiva Oa it is. Except for one little problem." She fumbles in her handbag, which she has kept on her lap during our lunch.

She holds up a tiny digital voice recorder. She mouths the words silently, "The first customer makes a deposit of $15,000."

"What is that thing," I ask her, "an Olympus?"

She smiles smugly, "Olympus digital with DSS Player Pro Software. Five hundred bucks. Not bad for digging someone's hole-in-the-ground."

"Mine's a Sony," I tell her, reaching into my breast pocket. "One of those old Microcassettes. About twenty-five bucks."

I mouth the words silently, "My husband doesn't know I'm having an affair."

She raises both hands palms up. "You know what I feel like every time I see you? I feel like I'm not really an adult. Like I don't have a job. Like working here is just an illusion. I also feel like sometimes my anatomy doesn't exist."

"I guess this is all for the best," I say, "because this way you and I won't waste any more time with each other. No more financial flirtations. I suppose this is how these…office relationships…these illicit affairs if you call them that…I suppose this is how they end."

The arrows on the TV are bobbing and jerking every which way, as if complicitous.

"No." She says. "You're wrong. This is how they begin."

Layoff

I'm not going to cry if they fire me,
she once said. Then she was out the door,
knocking the folders off her desk
as she passed. She turned and bent down
to pick them up one by one. I should smile,
she said, choking back the tears, right?
This is the best thing that's
ever happened to me, she said, looking like a
cormorant with wild eyes—wild eyes and
heavy feathers
kicking deeper into the lake.

The screen saver was still going
after she left.
Colored gliders soared across green mountains,
bouncing off the edges of the screen.
Secretly, the director adores me, she once said.

Landlocked

Twice a day
the equilibrium shifts.
The tide runs up the bay
into the river,
then the river runs out
into the bay.
Twice a day
birds rise and settle,
an osprey ascends
on a swift wind.
Half asleep, I dream—
or think I dream—of dairy cows,
dairy cows who used to graze on the salt grass
of the submissive tidal flats. If time were like the tide,
we would surge into the future
then rush back into the past
twice daily, with the present
only the expectation or regret
of the equilibrium shifting,
and if the river could type,
this is how it would sound:
a soft rush and whisper of keys
on a flat surface,
a current of brisk sighs.

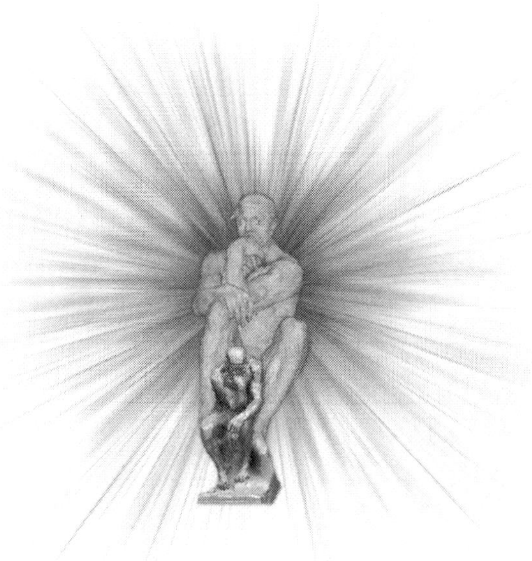

La Porte de l'Enfer
Auguste Rodin

Musee D'Orsay
Paris

une oeuvre maudite

Gates of hell
bolted shut,
tamper proof.

tamper-proof

tamper-proof

tamper-proof

tamper-proof

tamper-proof

We enjoy hell

Hell makes our faces glow

Porte de L'Enfer

Hell makes us sentimental

Hell makes us teary-eyed

Hell makes us pensive

Gates of Paradise

Gates of Hell

Hell makes us passionate

gates of hell
gates of paradise

bolted shut
tamper-proof

Satan appears

"You look wrecked, people, totally wrecked"
- Satan

La Porte de l'Enfer

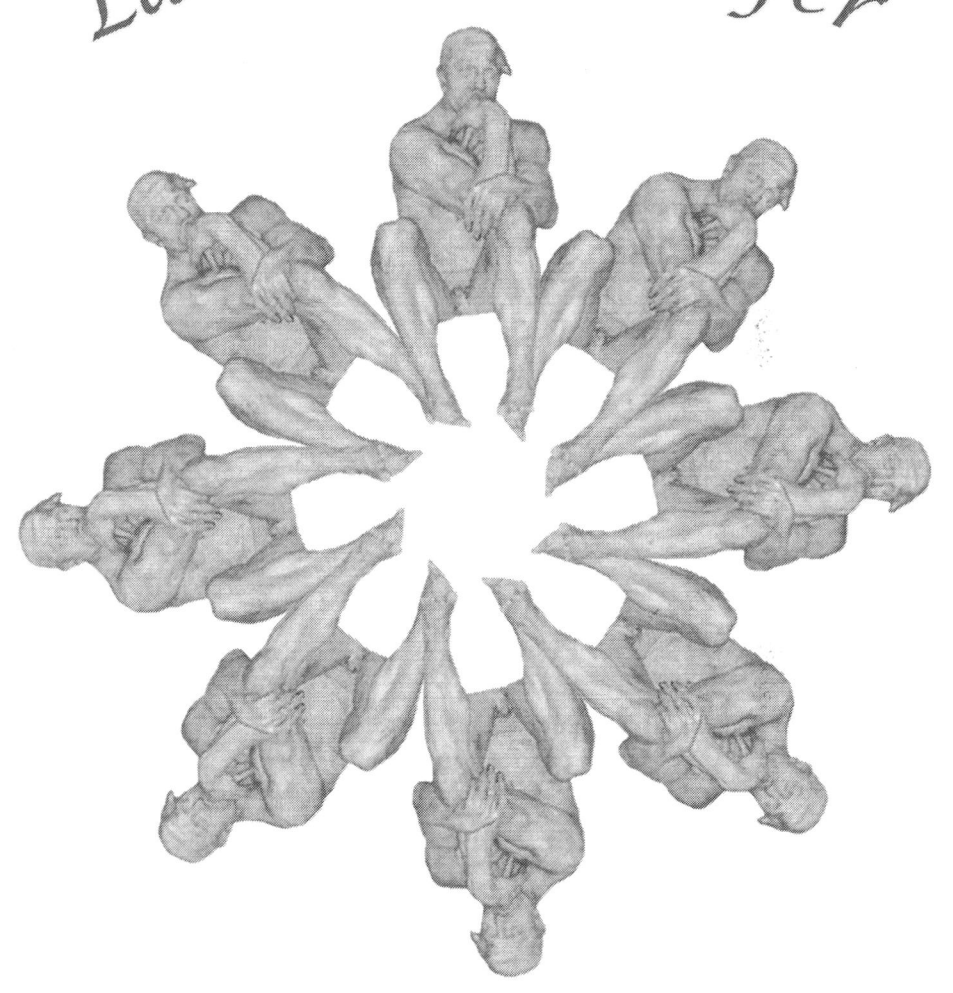

Auguste Rodin

Musee D'Orsay
Paris
une oeuvre maudite

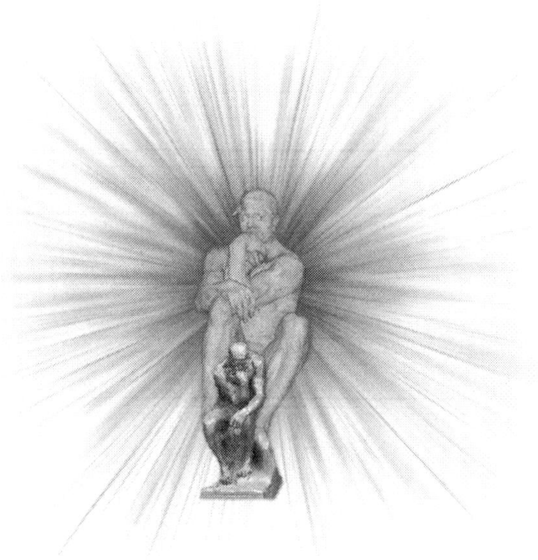

Two Birds, One Stone

I hadn't seen my wife for five years, and suddenly --- there she was. She was sitting at a table no more than twenty feet away.

We were in The Greenery—a singles' bar in Boston's Faneuil Hall---a huge cavernous space where parakeets squawked in overhead cages that hung from a greenhouse roof. The place was filled with plants, glass, and mirrors. It smelled of Windex.

I immediately averted my face, burying it in my hands; I peered out between my fingers. I wondered if I could escape the bar where I sat, past the table where she sat, without being noticed. What would she say, finding me alone in a singles bar?

But then, what would I say, finding her alone? As long as I could remain unseen, this might be a perverse form of entertainment. I relocated myself into the middle of a busy cluster of drinkers. Now I could watch her clearly in the mirror behind the bar, while maintaining an anonymous position in the audience.

She didn't seem to be waiting for anyone, but she seemed to be known to the waiters. They called her by name (Louise), everyone seemed happy to see her, and one of the waiters, as he leaned over to serve her a glass of something reddish, put his hand on the small of her back. At this touch, a dark and thoughtful look came over his face, as if he felt immortal longings.

Louise looked terrific. Her chin was always a little quick, but now the overall effect was sensual and aristocratic. So I thought many years ago, and so I thought now. Her delicate wire glasses set off her hair, which had faint beginnings of gray. The gray gave off light, suggesting a hairdresser's frosting, and she pulled several strands down over her eyes and peered through them at the retreating waiter. The only discordant effect was her skirt. Black and pleated, it looked a bit like a mourning shroud, and it so offset her mildness and stealthy grace that it made me uneasy.

I remembered the evening we met here, and how fresh and ceremonious this bar used to seem when we would visit it years ago. Every surface would be shining in the light, and the light that fell on our shoulders now was the same light that had fallen on us many years ago. Louise would come in with snow in her hair, a bright new dress, and good news, worries, or an apology for being late. After the separation I stopped coming, but lately I'd been coming back more often.

Three men approached her in a herd. They were well-dressed and blown-dry, radiating a brutish heat and audacity. They surrounded her and she disappeared from my line of vision. One man sat down and began to fill her ear with words, while another looked around for a waiter.

I remembered our last quarrel. How trivial it seemed. She left our apartment, driving off in the Honda. Her departure was meant to be final, but she had left twice before and I watched her go each time with a feeling that was far from happy, but also with that renewal of self-respect, of self-possession, that is often the reward for accepting a painful truth. It was summer and I was glad, in a way, that she had picked this lazy time to leave. Summer seemed to spare us the immediate necessity of legalizing our separation. We had lived together, off and on, for several years. I guessed she was content to let things ride until September. I guessed she would get the condominium. I liked the place and thought of that summer as the last days I would spend there.

At first, I didn't sleep very well in the empty bed. I didn't know how to deal with sleeplessness. If it was raining, I listened to the rain and thunder. If it wasn't raining, I listened to the distant noise of traffic on the Massachusetts Turnpike. I waited for divorce papers, but they never came.

I had a job with the state agency that oversaw community development and renewal. I took another job that promised me more money, but it didn't last long and I found myself out of work. It didn't bother me; I still had money in the bank and it was easy to borrow from friends. Maybe my indifference was due to an excess of hope. I had the feeling that I was still young and that the best years of my life lay before me. It was an illusion back then that I couldn't escape. I felt as if Louise had only driven the Honda over to the Lechmere Shopping Center to buy pillowcases. She'd be back. I'd get a new job. There was all the time in the world.

The noise level in the bar began to rise as evening approached. The great sheets of overhead glass were filled with a darkening blue, then turquoise, then black with a wavering blur of lights from the high windows of buildings that loomed over Faneuil Hall. The parakeets in their overhead cages looked bored and fell silent.

The three men who had surrounded Louise moved on. I glanced over my shoulder, just to make sure the mirror was accurately reflecting events. She must have told them she was waiting for someone. Or perhaps she said something that forced the prowlers on to their next event. She might have said nothing at all. I noticed she had a book in her hands, which she studied with fastidious absorption and which could hardly have been possible to read in the dim light.

Maybe now?

I could walk by her table, turn, and say, "Louise, what are you doing here?"

The pitch was off. What are you doing here? No. Not a good line. It might provoke an answer I didn't want to hear. Was I starting to feel something? A slight tremor of posessiveness?

A tall man arrived, leaned over and kissed her on the cheek. Then he sat down, as if he owned the chair and Louise as well.

He wore a moustache that dangled like frayed rope from each side of his mouth. His hair was pulled back in a ponytail tied with a blue ribbon, although he was bald on top. He was dressed in a yellow leisure suit and wore a pair of black cowboy boots. When he sat down next to her, Louise leaned toward him. Now all I could see in the mirror were the backs of their heads and Louise's elbows that assumed various positions—on the table, at her sides, in the air gesturing, or cupped by her hands.

Here is a woman who is having an affair, I thought. I swallowed my drink in one great gulp, the ice knocking against my teeth. With this oddly dressed character there, I decided it would be a good time to stop over, say hello, pause briefly and then move on to the rest of my unplanned evening. Mr. Ponytail would offer psychological protection. Louise and I wouldn't have to really talk.

The alcohol spreads through me, warming my imagination. I approach them. Maybe I do have to talk, briefly. But what if it's about me? If I sit down at their table and we begin to banter, it won't be long before her companion asks if I'm really her husband.

"Hiya, husband," he says. I can see his bony hand darting out like a chicken claw, as Louise moves to block it.

"Forget it," she says, looking at him with a vexed and rebuking expression.

Her friend and I are both standing now. I throw back my fist as if to hit him, and as he throws up his hands to protect his face, I kick him in the groin. Down he goes. A large man, thinking I've been attacked, rises from a nearby table, wipes his mouth with a white napkin, and strides over to where Louise's friend lies whimpering on the floor. He jumps on him with both feet. Somebody yanks me from behind and I feel a searing pain in my jaw and crumple down to the floor. I sit there rubbing my face, as the whole room begins to swarm around, fists flying, loud shouting. I see a body sliding across the floor and into the salad bar, where glass, ice, and vegetable shards explode around him. I hear a crash, and all the greenhouse windows of the huge brawling room come apart, raining glass, flower pots, baskets, and parakeet droppings on the brawling, screaming crowd. Police sirens in the distance tell me to seize Louise by the wrist and together we escape into the night.

I shook my head and glanced away from the mirror to where she was sitting. Her friend had left—for the men's room or forever? She was alone, at least for a while, staring at her unreadable book. I noticed two shopping bags, one on each side of her chair, large and crumpled as if she had just returned from an excursion at Lechmere.

Some things hadn't changed. When we lived together, she was always bringing shopping bags home. They would contain materials for projects—endless projects—fabric for quilts and books on quilt making, plants that would remain unwatered for weeks at the kitchen window. The bags might contain swatches of wallpaper, newspapers with uncompleted crossword puzzles, large balls of yarn, embroidery frames, a plastic cup containing an unfinished sundae, six new blouses—all of them the wrong size—cat food, dirty socks, and plastic bottles labeled for different feminine purposes but each containing the same white, gelatinous liquid.

There she sat, her eyes fixed on an unreadable book in a parody of erudition, lunatic transactions of the flesh being negotiated all around her, and two outrageous shopping bags resting at her feet. My annoyance arrived as vividly as the tremor of attraction had possessed me earlier.

Imagine my brain aflame with alcohol, as I drop down onto my hands and knees. I crawl across the floor to where she sits. I growl softly.

She keeps reading the book until she feels my stare scraping against the edges of her brain. I tug at the hem of her dress.

"Excuse me. Have you seen my Nobel Prize?"

"Nobel? Are you looking for somebody?"

"It's a small metal box filled with $100,000 in Swedish kroner. I must've dropped it on my way to the salad bar."

"Oh," she says, looking down with a mixture of impenetrability and contempt. "Sorry, I ate it."

Years ago, when I visited this bar, I would sit by myself staring into the fluttering darkness with its millions of tiny, dancing dots, while the shadows of men and women drifted through the silver smoke. This was the 1970s and smoke drifted in and out of buildings and people with abandon. Before laptops, there were only attaché cases with thick, neat accordions of computer paper inside, which you would raise gradually to eye level. No one could work ostentatiously or even frivolously in a darkened public space like a bar or coffee shop. Leisure suits were squalid garments made of stretchable double-knit polyester too dreadful to describe.

Of course, I am no longer a young, urban professional—yuppies we were called—sitting in a smoke-filled singles bar in Boston looking for some action, while elaborately pretending to be detached. I am an aging man living in Amherst, Massachusetts, and I am sitting on my front porch trying to write this while swatting at wasps with a rolled-up newspaper. I can see the Pelham hills from where I sit, and two hot air balloons are hovering over the cornfields. One of the balloons is rising above the other, slowly and with dignity, as if trying to escape. So help me God, it gets more and more preposterous, trying to pose as a young person in a singles bar in Boston. The term "swinger" isn't even used any more. There must be another word for it, but I asked my teenage daughter and she couldn't update the word --- the concept, really --- for my needs. I wonder if the present time wouldn't make more of a story than all this reminiscence. The force of life could be centrifugal, throwing a person further and further away from his purest memories. But back to the greenery and to Boston.

I ordered another beer and drank it quickly. When I glanced back over my shoulder, Louise was no longer at the table. She had become nothing more than a wavering filament of smoke rising from an ashtray. The shopping bags were still there. They lay heavily on each side of her empty chair. Messy newspapers stuck out of the top of the white one. The gray one looked like a large eroded stone that seemed ready to crumble into dust, as if it had been carried around for years. Looking at them was irritating, and my irritation increased as someone roughly tried to push in next to me at the bar.

"Hi there," the woman's voice said. "Couldn't help noticing you here." The voice had an anxious tone that might have been saying both, "I'm glad to see you," and "What's your problem?"

"Do you mind if I push in here for a minute?" Louise said. "If I keep sitting over there waiting to get served it'll be, like, like, the year 2013 and I'll be dead."

"Sure, move on in," I said. My neck felt warm. She was right against me, and I could feel the softness of her black sweater. She wore a silver chain around her neck, with a hollow silver heart as a pendant. Not the kind of thing I would have given her. As she stood and waited, the way she looked directly ahead of her, so that our view of each other in the mirror was shared, made us seem like innocent strangers.

What are you doing here? No.

Been awhile. No.

How's tricks, Louise? No.

How's life treating… No.

"Can I buy you a drink?"

"Sure," she turned to me. "How've you been? How's tricks? Been awhile."

"I'm fine," I said. "Tired."

"Still working in that grim, black building?"

I nodded as I ordered her a… "What do you drink these days?"

"Red devils."

"Red…?"

"Jamie knows. One-third vodka, one-third pernod, one-third grenadine. And some pretzels. Right, Jamie?"

"Hi Louise," the bartender said. "Instead of pretzels, you want to try our rice crackers with chive-dill dip?" He pushed a tray at us and watched her as she chewed. He looked as if he thought he was handsome.

She stood beside me, still looking into the mirror.

"You're tired too? My feet are killing me," she said.

"Feet? When do they hurt?"

"All the time. They hurt when I stand up, and I've been standing on them all day. They even hurt when I sit down."

"Do they hurt when you walk?"

"When I walk, I'm usually standing up. So, yes, they hurt when I walk. I walk all day. All that job hunting. Walking the streets. But this is getting pretty self-centered. Let's talk about your feet."

Her drink arrived, a bright-red concoction.

"I've got to go back there and sit down. Not that it will make my feet feel any better. You're welcome to join me."

At the table she held her drink and quietly watched the people at the bar. I let my gaze follow, and when I looked back her glass was empty. She wasn't even swallowing anymore.

"You're staring at me," she said.

"Yes, I am."

"Why?"

"A person can look," I said. "Don't I…?

"…know you from somewhere? Have you turned into one of those creeps? Picks up women at bars, takes them home, ties them up, and takes pictures."

"I don't mind. We could do that."

"You look the part, though. Maybe it's your suit," she said. "You don't look quite on the up-and-up in that suit. Sure, you have to wear it to work, but it's not really you, is it?" She sucked at the edge of her empty glass. The sucking seemed to restore her peace of mind. "I guess you're okay, though," she said distantly. Then she turned and smiled. "Don't try anything, though. I've got this new tear gas pen in my pocketbook."

She fumbled in her handbag and held up a small, shiny cylinder. "This is new. They're all the rage."

"Put that thing back," I told her. "They go off."

"They're supposed to." She rested it on the table. "What do you do, now? You look like you've turned into the kind of person that does something."

I explained to her about the bank and workout loans for failing investments, but I knew her eyes would begin to glaze past me even before I started.

"I'm sorry," she said. "That's just one of the questions I have to ask you. When I speak to men in bars, when we get to the part where I ask them what they do, I rush things as they talk to me. I fall in love with them, we marry, they're going blah-blah-blah, then we find ourselves in a bitter fight, separated, blah-blah, we hope to work things out. Then I find out their names, but there's already too much history between us. With you it's different. You wouldn't be concerned about my trying to get my talons into you, right? No danger of my trying to snare you, own you, provide a running commentary on your character defects. No chance of that, am I right?"

"Not a chance," I agreed.

"Are you embarrassed being here? Now that we've…met?"

Of course I lied to her, and of course she saw through it. I said, "Most of these blah-blah-blah men are married I suppose."

"It doesn't matter. Even if you don't know who in the world to love, it's important to choose love as a belief, a faith, isn't it? The particular person doesn't matter, does it? When I told you I hated you, for which I apologize, by the way, we hadn't been married that long, I discovered you wanted love, but not intimacy. You always talked to me as if you'd just met me at a bar an hour before, asking me things about myself you already knew."

I wondered if I were the kind of married man she could have an affair with. She must have been skilled in the marvelous skullduggery of illicit love, the passed notes, the phony telephone calls, the affected indifference, and the various closed doors of motels, friends' apartments, bed and breakfast cottages. It seemed possible.

Her thin black sweater, with the silver chain and pendant across the front, began to sting my eyes. She appeared different, in small immeasurable details, from the person who lay quarantined in my imagination. The crest of hair across her forehead was flecked with real grey—not the work of a hairdresser at all.

"And another thing," she said, and she was laughing, "I'm twenty-nine, in case you're trying to figure me out. I married young. And my husband doesn't understand me."

"Husbands never do. What are you reading? Could I take a look?"

She held up the book: *Sex, Sin and Shame in Hawthorne's Early Works.* "I've got plenty more books in my bag if you want to borrow them. Take two if you like."

"No thanks, I'm trying to quit."

"They're for this course I'm taking. At the Institute, The Institute for Personal Potential. That's what they call it. Potential. Like it? Potential?"

"Is that where they taught that the particular person you're in love with doesn't matter, as long as you're in love?"

"They never said that. I said it."

"Is that the place where they assign books on sex, sin, and shame to further your sense of personal potential?"

I couldn't tell if her behavior was due to Red Devils, but I was happy just to sit and listen to her talk. She told me about people in the bar, the well-dressed hookers who always sat in the corner, the men in gray suits who always seemed to own hotel chains.

"One of them wanted to marry me, but no way. I told him I was married, which was partly true, and I told him, hey, I need my independence. Marriage. Independence. You can't kill two birds with one stone anymore.

Once you lose yourself, it's hard to get yourself back. You can't even kill one bird with another bird. You know what I mean?"

I didn't. I didn't have any idea what she meant. Was she speaking of marriage as a stone, a burden? I had some ideas about stones myself. It was as if—throughout your life--- stones begin to gather inside you, at the very center of your life. These stones mean that certain things in your life can never be changed. You go on, you struggle, you try to earn a living. You try to pretend the stones aren't piling up inside you, since they never show on your X-ray. Those hard places, I imagined, existed somewhere around the guts and the heart. In some people they were great, dense things. I hadn't worked out the anatomical part too carefully, but that's what I imagined. Anyway, when I discovered this, I tried not to discuss other people's stones with them. I tried to never say anything harsh or critical to anybody about anything. But I could often feel their stones, just the same. Now I tried to guess the sizes and shapes of Louise's stones. Maybe there was only one.

My thoughts were going the wrong way, and I was starting to feel woozy and sleepy. I was losing complexity, like those brutish guys who had accosted Louise earlier, so straightforward that two seconds before they did anything, you could see each gesture coming. I wondered how long it would be before each of us would have to move into position, trying to defend our lives.

"Dickie?"

"......?"

"I've been talking to you. Did you hear me?"

"Sure, keep going."

"I don't work now," she was saying. "I'm kind of desperate."

"We really don't have to talk about this," I said. But she went on.

"At the Institute they say I'm full of energy, but I'm apathetic. You know what I mean?"

"......"

"Very little appeals to me. I guess I'll be starting one of those minimum-wage jobs pretty soon. But nothing appeals to me, as they say at the Institute."

"......"

"I mean, I'm smart, I'm not a loser. My problem is the pointlessness of certain things. A lot of things. I don't get the point. I want to help people, heal people, but how many jobs let you do that? If you're not a nurse or a doctor? I used to think I was a challenge to any psychiatrist. Now I have to take a self-esteem course. They give it at the Institute. That's so I can—they put it like this—learn to love."

She fiddled with her glass, her eyes cast down.

Love? God damn it, I thought. She used to live right in the middle of loving without giving reality a moment's thought. The shadows of her mind never threatened to turn on her and overpower her. Love? Something you learn to do? At an Institute? Though she hadn't stood up yet, her departure seemed to be already happening without me.

"One of the things they say? About learning to love? Keep a journal."

"A journal. You mean a diary? As in 'Dear Diary'?"

"It helps you cope with your failure. They say failure is important. It gives you a lot of really great information about yourself. There's this psychologist? At the University of Texas? He studied middle-aged engineers who'd lost their jobs. Those who kept journals were more likely to find new jobs…because writing about their feelings made them come to terms with getting laid off. It increased their social skills by making them less bitter."

"How many Texas engineers are we talking about here?"

"Not only that, some of them wrote personal histories and memoirs based on the journals."

"And you're going to do this?"

"I don't know, I don't know," she said, "but who can say that I shouldn't? What harm would it do?"

"At college," I said, "I wrote a couple of memoir chapters for a course. You know what my professor said? He said there are two problems with every memoir."

"Two problems?"

"Yes. The first problem is 'so what'?"

"What's the other one?"

"The second problem is 'who cares'?"

"I care." She seemed to be startled, at first, by her own intensity. Gradually, she began to look more committed.

I thought of her trying to repeat our lives in writing, trying to mimic our whole history with incongruous and mangling words, thanks to the inspiration of The Institute for Personal Potential.

Suddenly she laughed. "Texas engineers!" She hit the table with the palm of her hand. It was not a sarcastic laugh, but a laugh full of wonderment, a full laugh that enjoyed a joke, the kind of laugh she was laughing the first time I saw her, many years ago.

"Isn't this great," she said. "What a coincidence. That we met here?"

I wanted to say yes, it's great. But the truth—the substance of the coincidence was that no, it was not. It was strange without being an occasion, an event. Before I could stop her, she leaned over to me, put her right hand squarely on my shoulder and looked at me sharply. When she straightened up she said, "We're going to make an evening of it, that's for sure. You're not going anywhere, am I right?"

"You're right. I'm not going anywhere. We could always go there together."

She started to collect her books from the table, and then she looked up.

"You know, time makes us change. You can't always be just a bystander, hiding out behind a potted plant in the corner of the bar. You've got to come out, you've got to look around…"

She dropped one of the books, which thudded next to the tear gas pen on the table, knocking it to the floor. The blast, the shattering sound, made my eyes leap open. A woman screamed. I could hear the shot echoing through the room, then the silence. The pen lay on the carpet, three inches from my right foot and the acidic odor that rose was surprisingly faint.

I sneezed. People began to murmur, and their voices rose like a chain of barking dogs. The drone of voices seemed unearthly. The bartender made his way over to us. It was a walk, a little stiff, where every step seemed to have been practiced, every step was a small melodrama.

Louise had her head down, hands over her ears. She was crying. "It was a mistake," she murmured. "Just a mistake." But the bartender gazed at her, appalled and frightened. "Really it was just a mistake," she repeated over and over. "This whole evening's a mistake. I'm embarrassed."

"You're embarrassed! I just lost six customers just now, right out the door."

"Just a mistake," Louise said softly through her tears. She groped through her purse, trying to find a tissue. The bartender grabbed her by the shoulders and began to shake her as if he were trying to wake her from a dream. Back and forth her head tossed.

"Out," he said. "Louise, out, out. Out."

I tried to laugh, but the scene was too crazed and despairing. The bartender looked as if he wanted to make a speech, like a parent. His face was tightening up, his jaw stiffened, but he didn't know how to start, didn't know how to choose his opening lines.

I tried to laugh again, wishing I could redeem the moment, but Louise didn't laugh. She ran off to the ladies' room.

What would they say about this at the Institute? I wondered.

When Louise returned, there was a set look in her eyes. She seemed to hear nothing.

That was all. It was over. I searched for my attaché case and my coat, paid the check at the bar, and headed off into the night.

Although I called her a couple of times after that evening, she seemed to have a different ending in mind, different from the one you are reading here. In her scenario, she didn't remember me at all. Beneath our banter at the bar there existed a powerful doubt that anything we did when we were married ever took place. To protect herself she wanted me to be a stranger again. She wanted to sit at her table and watch me walk into the bar. I would take my seat and pretend not to see her. She would pretend not to see me, as well. Clouds of silver smoke would drift around us, like the weather in some bewildering dream—a dream where the past was familiar but flexible, where you could almost touch it, mold it like clay, make it soft—a palpable thing only trying to be helpful.

BETWEEN MY FINGER
AND MY THUMB

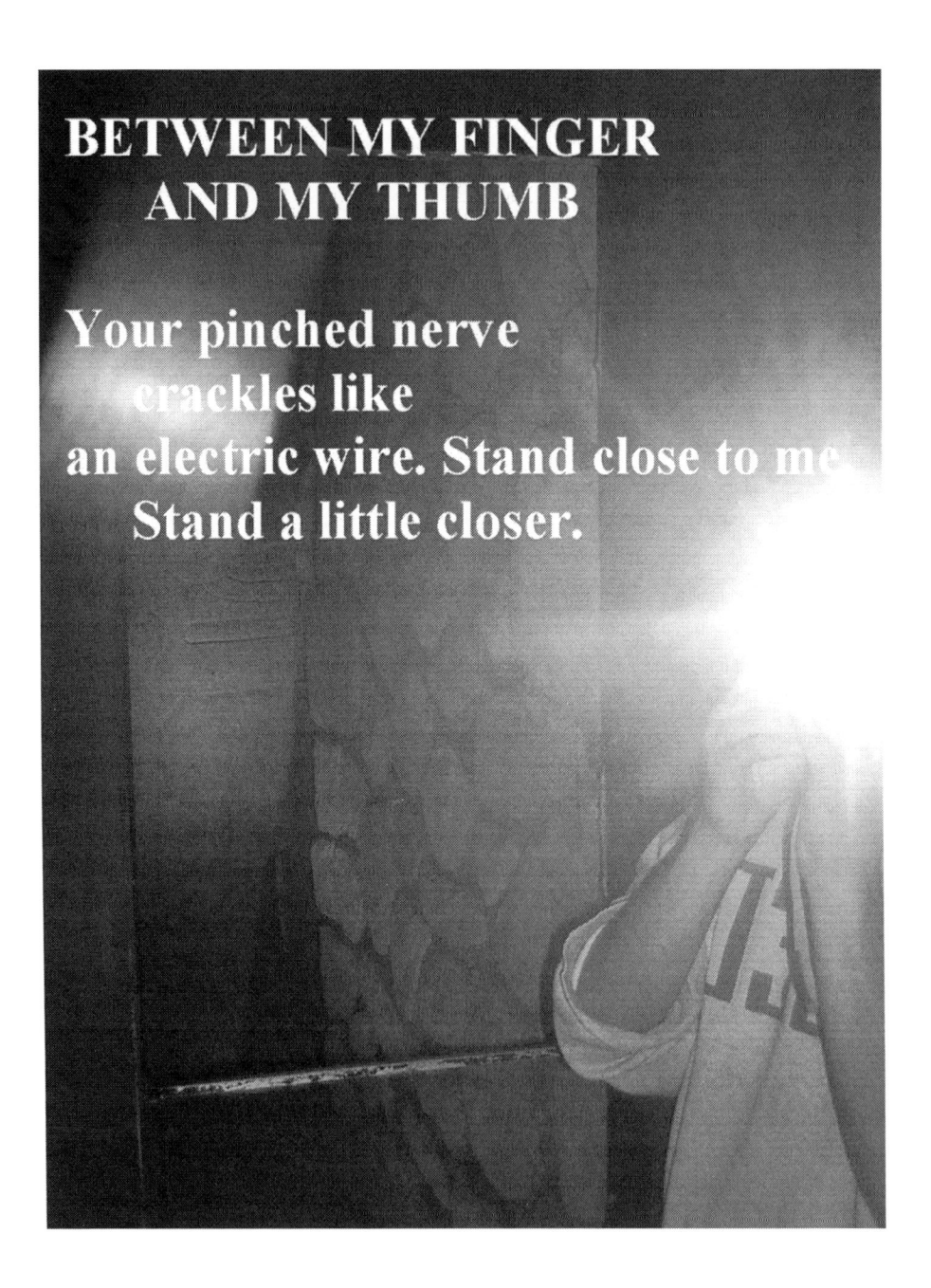

Your pinched nerve
 crackles like
an electric wire. Stand close to me.
 Stand a little closer.

Carpathians

There are countries of the spirit,
Where the villages are lit by torches
And the bears weigh 700 pounds.
The clocks are sad
And strike the wrong hours
While park benches are as empty as the sky.
The tyrannical government
Lies about the weather,
Lies about the sun, moon, stars,
Sex and the mists off the river. The
streets are named Liberation Avenue,
Redemption Boulevard, and Square of
The Sixteenth of January.
This is the world we ran to from the world
While storms of cursing exiles fled the other way
And a father loomed above us all—
Loomed like a mountain range.
A Carpathian father ready to drink the blood of humans.
Seeking counsel I ask,
"Can my father really
Be mastered through
The interpretation of dreams?"
The therapist replies,
"According to Cornell Medical School's
Malaise Inventory, someone who is disturbed
May also have a genuine complaint."
The doctor has a pleasant if inexpressive face
And a disarming manner.
You can see
A fine lucid intelligence in his eyes.
"You must be very confused," the doctor says.
You nod.
"How lonely it must be having your condition.
How baffling and troublesome and unfair."
You bow your head silently in acknowledgment.
Like most educated people,
You are conversant with the basic
Tenets of the therapeutic relationship,
Issues of transference and countertransference

And so forth,
So you do not wish to acknowledge
The fact that you wish with all your heart
To embrace the man, to clamber up
The cliffs of his soaring Carpathian lap,
And remain there
Until you are healed.

Earth Rising

From an asteroid in empty space
An image of the earth rising
Would compel watchfulness:
And the glory of
The earth could be known
By its continents
Unless the oceans become colorless
Because the sky has disappeared.
No more sky, it is theorized,
Means no more earth.
To verify, the Kepler team
Has asked the NASA group
For an analysis, and the Director
Of the Astrophysics
Subcommittee of the
NASA Advisory Council's
13-member group has promised
To undertake the study
But has cautioned against
"False Positives" as to
The asteroids that
Hold the pale sky together,
And keep the earth
In place.

Onlooker

She is, he estimates, thirty-five or forty.
She must have been married once,
or maybe twice.
Her past is, at this point,
none of his business.
She walks
on the sunny side of the street,
she wears a suit,
probably a little perfume.
She looks in the store windows:
jewels,
suits,
dresses, hats,
antiques,
gloves,
shoes,
embroideries,
paintings,
everything that is for sale
charms her,
charms him.

She enters a building, the doorman nods,
the elevator ascends smoothly to his desire.

A Place Where You're Known

You can always book a table,
It's not the most expensive place in town,
But the most expensive place where you're known.

The other guests are just as well known as you.
If there were a headwaiter he would greet everyone
Just as warmly.

You take a chair, and look around at
The ecclesiastical meeting room, the place
Where rummage sales are held, nativity plays performed.

Forty of you, men and women, listening with attention
To a speaker at a podium. The faces of the young, the old,
The haggard, and the serene convey no anonymity

But instead a lively mixture of nationalities and races
That some would say has made our country great.
I'll join you now, pull up my own chair.

We are mental scavengers
Extracting rocks and pebbles within ourselves.
Well known for what we share of love and failure.

Snowstorm In Eden

The first whisper of snow
At the gates, every creature
Wants out. Shuddering. Murmuring.
Snow falls on the Garden's clipped hedges,
Topiary shrubs, and the dwarf peach trees
Nailed to their trellises.
Martyred lovers, the blizzard is coming on.
You see it descending, circling,
Here within the lush garden
Of childhood.
High winds, whiteout, squall.
That tree is already rising,
Raging like music.
The Opera of the Angels is finished.
The applause is fading.

The cheerful authority
  of the
sky's creased
  and frozen expression,
    Crammed in   carcasses
A forgotten earth
  Muddying   flat
Beneath the layers
        of rock

Ants

A solitary ant, when closely seen,
Is quite unlike a thinking, sentient being.
Observed in nettly field or tangly lawn,
It looks more like a goofy ganglion
Or nervous neurons legging o'er the lea
With deaf, dumb, blind yet restless energy.

But should this ant encounter on its way
A sickly moth expiring in the hay,
Observe how swiftly ants as one unite,
Soon four or ten have taken up the fight.
The queasy moth, encircled, has no chance
When pushed around by avid, addled ants.

Soon hundreds more arrive from near and far.
This blackened blob of living caviar,
This antsy broth that froths around the moth
Is purposeful as Hun or Visigoth
The day that ancient Rome was sacked and wrecked
By one totalitarian intellect.

The mass becomes a planner, calculator.
The moth becomes another meal to cater.
Does this reflect the mind of the Creator?

An ant's not intellectually reflective.
Its brain is most effective when collective.
Some call this outcome "naturally selective."

If so, is ant or moth the saint or sinner?
With natural selection there's no winner
When everyone is someone else's dinner.

Perhaps we've stretched the metaphor too far,
Imagining an antsy avatar,
With mortal man an insect's supplicant
And Deity descending as an ant.
These questions cover ground already trod.
The answer's up to Darwin, or to God.

Christmas In Amherst, Mass.

In a town I know of
it is always cold.
The people—the Valley People—
sleep in barns resting their heads on cow-plops, and the mothers
speak to their children down the chimney. Wild dogs scavenge in
the Dumpsters behind the mall
and the insides of the wood houses
are dark and smokey. Once a year these
superstitious folk
hang crude evergreen icons that they have sawed off
from somewhere that proclaim
"'Tis the season to be jolly," but it isn't really,
as candles sputter over mantles, garments of clothing
from severed feet dangle at the chimneys.
To the Valley People, the devil is real, in his
sheepskin suit dyed red, entering
down chimneys to avoid the wreaths of garlic and turnips the people
hang by their front doors. After the devil has filled his sack
with sweet rot from the larders of the Christian people,
up the chimney he rises with the spoils,
riding off behind wild animals to assignations
with wolves, witches, and corpses.
Life in this town is nasty, brutish, and short,
the way conservatives like it.

Dec. 6, 1984

My love is a house on fire,
Burning into my spirit.

I close my eyes and hear the blaze rage,
I catch the rooftop's crackle.
Someday she'll lift her empty spoon
From the highchair
To catch the embers.

She came from far away, trillions of light years away,
Before her birth sent her crashing into the kitchen like a comet.
Eternity is endless even in a universe so young,
But we're catching up.

In The Cafeteria

It's not on the menu
This lack, this gap.
Who will sit beside me?
What shall we eat?
There's no milk in the machine
No noodles
Green peas roll off my tray
Like beads
There's sauce on my chin
The heart can't drag itself
Fast enough
So I escape to help the art teacher
Set out new jars of white paste
One kid always eats his
Then smiles wisely.

Leaving Chicago
(Excerpt from memoir)

May 1973.

I was thirty-six years old and no girl, no woman, no man had ever propositioned me on a first date, but here she was, leaning forward slightly from the edge of the sofa, saying, "Now what do we do?"

She wore a purple evening dress and her dark hair meandered down over her shoulders. Her chin was in her hand, and on her face was a faint smile, as if she were contemplating something that she would laugh at later.

I was hesitant. I felt more comfortable with the whispered innuendo, the lowered eyelids, a foot underneath the table --- a soft stocking slowly moving up and down the calf.

Had I understood her correctly? I said nothing.

"Well?" she said.

We'd been to a dance at the Central Park Zoo. I felt the wheel of my life turning, bringing up dreams and desires from eight years before --- a dance at Chicago's Lincoln Park Zoo. Daphne Harwood (mahl *) and I were pictured in the newspaper. Daphne looked on lovingly while I held an orangutan in my arms. The zookeeper looked pleased at his animal's conduct. The monkey house had been made into a discotheque, and all the monkeys watched their cousins with forbearance as we twisted, turned, and jerked our bodies to the music. The orangutan, according to the zookeeper, was named "Lady Jane." The others were Caesar, Cleopatra and Sinbad. Each of the animals displayed long reddish hair and hooked hands and feet. Lady Jane reached over to scratch my back, then squirmed in my arms while the newspaper photographer urged us on. "Great! Great Wonderful! Go at it, you two!"

Is farce an aphrodisiac? In Chicago, Daphne and I had visited the monkey house. In New York, this new woman and I visited the lion house. I tried to keep the lions, and the woman, from intimidating me, but it didn't seem to matter which house or zoo you visited or in what city. All creatures, great and small, seemed to promise love and adventure.

"I have to fly up to Rochester tomorrow." I said. Now, it seemed, we were playing chicken. I quickly explained that Rochester was a long flight, and that the plane left in the morning, from New Jersey, only five hours from now.

"That's plenty of time," she said.

Chimps Not So Nutty

By Lois Baur

AFTER ONE LOOK at the nonsense going on outside their bars last night in the Lincoln Park zoo, Sinbad, Caesar, Cleopatra, Lady Jane, and their compatriots in adjoining apartments were glad they were protected by steel bars.

One glance at some of their distant relatives peering at them from under peculiar haircuts and bald pates—one look at the couples dancing round as tho they had just escaped from the same jungle —that's all the inmates of the monkey house needed to retire to the darkest corner of their apartment and contemplate. Or look wildly for the protection of their keeper.

As A. Bradley Eben said: "They look out at us as tho we're nuts—and we are!"

This was the scene at the Lincoln Park Zoological society's second annual black tie soiree in the zoo—a party so popular 600 paid $35 a couple and there were two dances, one in the lion house to a live band, a second in the monkey house, a discotheque where people on the outside recognized cousins several times removed on the inside.

Lady Jane, a lovable orangutang, brought out by her keeper to meet some admirers, went for everyone with open arms. Dick Bently and Daphne Harwood seemed to be her favorites.

Jo-Jo, the neurotic yellow baboon, looked at Kellogg Fairbanks III and Sarah O'Shaughnessy and Tracy Brown and Dick Banz going thru strange wiggling, twisting, turning, jerking movements on the dance floor. Then he mimicked them, twisting, turning, jerking—trying to match their neuroses. Then, in obvious hysteria, Jo-Jo turned his back politely and shook with uncontrolable giggles, his hand to his face.

• BABY ORANGUTANG Lady Jane climbs into arms of Richard Bently at the Lion House ball in the Lincoln Park zoo last night. Daphne Harwood looks curiously at the favorite character at the soiree put on by the Lincoln Park Zoological society—with dancing in both the monkey house and lion house. Party was so popular that 600 paid $35 a couple to attend the second annual event.

She lived at 9 West 73rd St., in a handsome brownstone built for Victor Herbert, the composer of romantic operettas from the 1890s. I knew his work well. Our record cabinet back home in Illinois was full of Victor Herbert one-sided records that we played on an old crank-up gramophone with a speaker horn shaped like a morning glory:

ALL RISE

On the beautiful isle of our dreams, dear,
Where there's never a sorrow or pain,
Ev'ry trouble and care quickly vanishes there,
And all is made happy again.

    I had always thought of Isle of Our Dreams as my special "seduction song" even though it was a waltz and very quaint and I had never really seduced anybody with it. One candidate shrugged it off as "syrupy" and another said it was "too idealistic" to elicit an erotic response.
    She lived in an apartment on the second floor, with French doors that opened onto a balcony with elaborate ironwork. At night I would pass by on the street below and I would see her shadow dancing on the walls, but I could never quite see her or what she might be wearing, if anything. I imagined myself as a phantom in the night, murky with a love she had yet to discover.
    I hardly knew her when I invited her to the Central Park Zoo dance. She accepted my invitation after I assured her that it would be a thrilling event and that I had danced with many zoo animals in the past, danced with them without incident.
    Now I asked her to dance, and we drifted delicately among the other couples like two people in a fine, amusing dream. Her smile had an unguarded sweetness, I thought, but her dark beauty was menacing; the kind of threat that can only bring on treacherous passion.

                              (from the memoir *Leaving Chicago*)

Lines Composed Upon The Brooklyn Bridge After An All-Nighter

Wind peels waves off the river
and heaps them against the pilings.
Gulls cry and dip low,
then shoot straight up again.
We wonder, why don't doormen
ever go to sea? Why don't nuns
pray before the great stone Buddha
up in the Bronx?

"Deliver us from the heavenly
beauty of the sunrise over Queens"

Our hearts are armored
with booze and grass,
and we ask the prayerful nuns
to intercede,
"Spare them the knowledge
of where they are going
when the bridge they cross
disappears in a thick rain."

The News

Open to me, says the world,
speaking in such clear-cut sentences
that I see beauty in its style.

I stand at the doorway,
ridiculous in pajamas.
What others find in art, I find in news.
What others find in human
love, I find in news, so very trouble-free.

Sunrise, a glaze of dampness
over every growing thing,
beads of cold light
formed on the orange wrapper.
Is there a voice here?

Open to me, says the world,
so that I can finally say
tomorrow and the day after and even
the future. News, the hailer, the healer,
the tutor—even more than beauty.

Death cannot harm me,
more then the news stirs me,
to cherished life.

Promised Land

Five-thirty in the afternoon on a hot Friday in August: It is always a long journey home on summer weekends, and I am making the trip less often now. I wear the usual dark blue dress, nondescript and corporate, and I carry the usual brown handbag. I have a small suitcase for overnight.

The trip starts underground, five stops on the Number Two from Wall Street to Penn Station. We stand in clusters where we expect the subway door to appear, straining over the platform's yellow danger line, gazing down the tunnel for the lights of the oncoming train. When the cars roar by in a hot wind, we recoil, and when the train stops we twist and squeeze past sluggish bodies while the loudspeaker squawks: Stand back and let 'em off.

Everything is familiar: the odor of salami and garlic on people's breath, the hurtling, side-to-side roll before we pull in at the graffiti-marked stop beneath Penn Station. The same mechanical voice: "Stand clear of the closing doors."

I change trains at Jamaica, the beginning of Long island The loudspeaker's voice becomes less cramped and commanding: It sings, "leaving for BALD-win, FREE-port, BELL-more, WAN-taugh, SEA-ford, Massa-PE-qua" but none of these pleasantly named towns is mine. My train doesn't go that far. My train heads south, sliding past places that don't have names—factories, storage buildings, machine shops—until I get closer to home, near the Sunrise Highway with its unsynchronized lights and its shopping centers, where carloads of local greasers cruise up and down the road all evening waving crude signs out the car windows and making faces. Nobody out here trusts Manhattan. They call it The City, as if Queens were The Country. I wanted to go to The City all my life, and so I went. Now, my father wants me to come back and live with him.

He has been a widower these past few months. A few neighbors have been sympathetic, but he has not been open to their compassion. There are two parts to him: the one that takes in everything clearly, and the one that stays back, withdrawn and hidden. Lately, he seems to have retreated to a place inside his head, thinking in a different language.

A man in a wrinkled business suit sits nearby, watching me. I open my handbag and look inside. It's filled with nothing, just small fragments of my life. A smile starts to play at the corners of my mouth. I have to tighten my lips to make it go away. Everything you do in life gets so mixed up with strangers you have to be careful, even just looking at them. It's safer to gaze out the window as the used car lots and funeral parlors slide by and think about what I'm going to say to my father. No. No, I'm not coming. Get someone else. Get Bobby and Melissa and their two teenagers. Get Helen to come back from California with her salesman. Get somebody else.

The man I've been seeing, Richard, thinks I'm being childish about it. "You're almost thirty years old. What's all the terrible conflict about?" He wants me to move in with him. He's The City. He's Manhattan, the glittery Manhattan. He says he's related to the Bush family. I ask him, "Cousins?" He says, "Distant." He is sweet and funny and easy to see through. He can also be kind.

This is the not-quite-suburbs. In spite of the distance, when I get off the train, I'm still within the city limits. The platform at the Rosedale station is a great concrete slab that leads to an arching bridge over the tracks. The bridge has wire mesh sides to prevent public atrocities. When the trains pass below, the noise of metal on metal blends with the surge of overhead jets as they descend into Kennedy airport, making a dreadful music.

For a few years my parents rented in East New York. Then they moved here—a step up the ladder. I guess that's what it means to be settled down—all the imagined journeys you trace for yourself across the maps and globes in a schoolroom reduced at last to just a daily commute, a repeated voyage past houses with lights on and people inside eating supper.

My father traveled farther. He came across the sea from Yugoslavia before the slaughter, long before the shells of the Serbian artillery. There was always puzzlement in his eyes as his family grew up around him. The older and noisier we became, the lonelier he seemed to feel. Perhaps we, too, were sort of an escape, his flight from the past without destiny or calling. Often, when I asked him about growing up in that distant country, he would lower his eyelids, turn down the corners of his mouth, and swat the air with one hand, as if the first part of his life had been an insect. So I had to imagine the country that he would never talk about, and all I could see was forlorn villages surrounded by waterfalls and wolves, where farming was still done by hand and people traveled everywhere in carts. Then I imagined the endless pop-pop of snipers in the hills, teenagers with their shoulder grenade launchers, closed shops, blasted buildings, listless walkers in shattered streets. My father said the family farm overlooked the sea, but this vision seemed too sunny for anything I could imagine. I suppose he had a childhood, but whenever I asked him about it he would struggle for an answer. "What do you want to know?" he would say.

I swing my suitcase up the front steps. Its weight provides enough momentum to carry me through the front door, and I slide it across the floor. My father's chair, in the kitchen, scrapes back and he emerges holding up his hand, looking at me the way people look through windows. Then he stops, slumps his shoulders, and stoops to pick up my bag. He wears his gray pants and shirt, with Tony stitched across the pocket. It is cleaned and pressed, but its metallic dullness, which matches the color of his hair, makes him look like a man stubbornly dedicated to sadness.

"What's new, Daddy?"

"Nothing. Stomach pains. And you?"

"I'm so glad to see you."

"Why are you looking around?"

He leads me upstairs, carrying my suitcase. Inside the house, piles of newspapers and mail cover every horizontal surface. With Mother gone, the rooms seem large and dim, the carpets heavier, the ceilings higher.

In my bedroom, my mother's primly shaped dresses are spread out across the bed.

"You should have those," my father says, setting down the suitcases. I can hear the labor of his breathing.

"Daddy, I've already looked through this stuff. The dresses are not my size. They're old-fashioned, I can't wear them." Saying this suddenly seems blasphemous. "I'm sorry, Daddy. I just can't wear them."

"You should go through them again. Make sure." He holds one of them up, shaking out the wrinkles. "If I put them in the Goodwill box, some punk just sets them on fire."

"What about the fur coat?" It's the only thing that remains in Mother's closet, next to several bottles of old perfume.

He frowns. "It's got a tear in the sleeve. But I keep it for a while. Maybe I find something else for you. I look around. Something in the metal box, maybe."

I cannot imagine what something else might be. The metal box is full of nothing but old papers: the deed to the house, my father's Yugoslavian passport with his picture in merchant seaman uniform. Nothing we have is of any value except for the coat, a new battery in the car, and an ancient lathe with worn out belts that he keeps in the basement (an awkward sentence). I can't use the battery or the lathe.

Next day, we're sitting on the front steps, each of us with a can of soda. I wish I could blurt it out, tell him I don't want to move back. I want nothing of my father's grip on the smallness of life, or the old people I've known since they were young, and the middle-aged people I knew when they were my present age.

The street is potholed, and the sidewalk in front of us is crumbling and cracked. Some local entrepreneur is building a duplex in the vacant lot across the street. In the day's heat, the workers remove their shirts, soak them in buckets of water, and squeeze them over their heads.

I'm like a child when I come to Rosedale, fearful of my father's judgment of me: a frivolous person. Richard says, "Love to come out there and meet your dad sometime." But it won't happen. Not ever. Richard is Manhattan.

He doesn't need me. I like that. It means he doesn't judge me. Is that love? If it is, it's a new kind of love for me.

If my father knew about him, he'd quickly see my lazy self-indulgence. That's how fearful I am. But only here, in this house, are my mind and energy drained by such fear.

My father's lips are pressed together now. He looks steely and quiet, his face expressionless, his eyes fixed and remote. He is thinking to himself in his native language.

The grass in the two small rectangles that front our house has turned brown. The workers across the street have their wet shirts hanging down from beneath their hard hats, like soggy burnooses. The studs of wood they are handling look warped from the heat, glistening with spots of resin.

"Daddy," I say carefully, "are you angry, are you sad that I don't come out here more often?" He is quiet. Then I say it, "Daddy, I'm not moving back here with you." There is an up-spin of relief, and then it is gone. The oak trees stir slightly, then we're caught again as a deafening jet thickens the air on its way to Kennedy.

His head lowers, then his face tips up and his eyes come into view, hardening.

"I'll be home on weekends more. I promise," I tell him.

I stand up, getting my blouse unstuck from my stomach and my skirt from the back of my legs. The big oak tree in front of the house casts a shadow that ripples across the hot gleam of cars passing in the street. I sit down again, watching the workers across the street, their dull hammering drowned out by the intermittent sound of jets.

It is a longer wait than I had anticipated for him to answer. The shadows seem to stretch out further as we sit here. We are going into the worst part of the afternoon.

My father moves his head from side to side, without removing me from his stare. I frown at my lap. I scratch at a spot on my blue skirt.

He gives me a long, shrewd stare. "But I understand," he says, in an alarmingly different voice. Everything is strained, unnatural. Then: "You sleeping with some guy?"

My ears start to burn. "Daddy, I'm going to live with some guy." My words seem blurred and indistinct. "I'm sorry if it bothers you. Is that enough? I'm sorry."

The heat and noise seem endless, draining us of everything but simple thoughts. It's too hot for feelings.

He presses his lips together, as if my answer is impertinent and slightly irritating. "You know something?" he says. "We moved out here twenty-five years ago. Twenty-five years ago, today."

He could live here for another twenty-five years, too. I could live with him, surrounded by the house he once ran (ran?) and would soon be running us, with its demands for paint and new plumbing, the dampness of its basement, the squirrels in the gutters, the moths beating night after night, with their big wings, at the window screens.

"Twenty-five years ago," he says. "Now everybody's moved away or died. Even D'Ambrosio's dying." He glances at the house next door with its drawn shades.

"But you've always hated him."

"I don't complain about him. I'm a happy man. I know something about laughter. You know who he is? One of the family."

"Family?"

"You don't know who the family is? You're such a baby. Half of Rosedale belongs to them. They keep order here. They help the cops. Smart people. You don't get money without being smart people. D'Ambrosio, he always wanted to be gunned down in some nice little restaurant off Mulberry Street. But look at him now, just dying behind the window shades."

I begin to think again of what it is going to mean, moving in with Richard. It is going to mean not being on my own. It's going to mean having someone to bitch at, someone to lean on, someone to tell me I am essential to his breathing and being. Lots of things seem better than that.

I listen to my father, polite but neutral now. Because I remain detached, he wants to tell me more: life in Queens, the way the neighbors looked down on him because he had an accent and wasn't Irish Catholic. When I say nothing for a long time, he adds, "Where will you go when this guy is through with you?"

It's as if I've been expecting the question all the time he's been talking, and with no answer prepared, I just lean forward, with my face and part of my body leaning over the steps, and say, "I'll go somewhere. I don't know where yet, but somewhere."

He edges back into the shadow of the porch. "I will go somewhere," I say, emphasizing each word carefully.

I cannot tell, by his hard gaze, whether he senses this feeling I have. But whatever purpose is emerging, he looks like he wants to grasp it for himself. Suddenly he starts forward and catches my arm. I watch his face as it is smitten by something I haven't thought to display before him, much less brandish: my youth. I can see that he wants it. His grip tightens on my arm, and it seems to strengthen this feeling.

I do not pull away from him. Then he inclines his head as if to accept responsibility for my frustration. Too weary to move, he stares at me and says, "The land." He clears his throat. "You should have it someday."

The dry leaves on the oak tree rustle. I do not understand what he is saying.

"I said I would look around for something to give you. Your mother's coat, no."

He gazes through his thoughts at the oak tree and continues. "Ten hectares. Karla writes me from Yugoslavia, 'When are you going to sign it over to us, Tony? You don't need it any more. We could add it to the farm.' But I never signed it over."

"Land?"

"On the hill near Kraljevica. It still belongs to me. It looks down on the sea. I never sign it over to Karla. Some day, maybe, you can see it yourself. I still have it. It's in the metal box upstairs. It's a deed, ten hectares. Maybe you can use it someday, maybe not. If not, then dream about it. It's yours."

That was all he said, as the heat continued to press into darkness. The construction workers across the street set down their tools and began to leave. A few moths appeared and we hoisted ourselves up and walked back into the house. The gathered heat of the day, sultry and depressed, was worse than the outside. The sweat sprang from my skin. I tried to force the windows higher in their sashes, but there was no breeze anywhere. No air.

I saw him standing in the living room, staring at the ceiling.

I was reminded, then, of how he would wait at the foot of the stairs for my mother when they went out, just the two of them, for an evening. My mother would walk about overhead, and I could hear her high-heeled shoes clattering as she moved from her bureau to her closet mirror. Her staccato footsteps, patternless at first, would become more purposeful as she stopped to pick out earrings or brush her dark hair. All at once she would march across the floor, and the sound of her shoes' percussion would burst out like a tap dance as she came down the stairway.

My father, as if signaled, would go to the hall closet for her fur coat. He would hold it out for her as she passed, and she would always say, "Tony, Don't you look terrific!"

Now, I tried to continue our conversation, but my father seemed exhausted. His gaze moved down from the ceiling, looked around the room. His head retreated into the collar of the shirt with Tony stitched across the pocket.

Suppose he was once a boy? What were the summers like? Maybe there were flowers and mulberry trees stretching across the ten hectares down to the Adriatic shore. Maybe he ran through fields of grass, but who wanted to remember? Those days and nights were all weighted down for him like stones. No one said it was poetry finding a promised land (awkward) or giving up an old land whose bitter memories kept him reaching doggedly ahead.

I usually do not believe things people tell me before nightfall. Only when there are cool and melancholy shadings in the air do their words become real. This was the only time, before he died, that my father ever mentioned this land as a legacy, this field somewhere on a hillside, in a country I will never see. But that night, he showed me the deed in the metal box, and that evening I set out on my travels. I may never possess this field as my own. But I might take a gentle step toward it and then, realizing that I am not alone, I might see, with Richard, the outlines of a new shore and strain in the sunlight to see it clearly.

Sunrise, a
    smaze of dampness over
every growing thing,
        beads of
    cold light
    formed   in a
wrapper.
this is called "read rage"
the voice fades
        Is there a voice here?
            hear
Is there a voice here?

Not There They're Not

My friend Earl Carlyle was talking. Earl's a minister over at that Grace Church next to the parking lot. This gives him the right to talk sometimes. The three of us were sitting at the kitchen table. A bottle of Chardonnay kept going around. There was Earl and me and Cecil Fisher. We were neighbors. Earl's wife, Sheila, left him a couple of weeks ago. Cecil's wife had been put away. An institution. My wife was at a buyer's convention in Vegas. So there were just the three of us. On a Saturday night. No women.

Cecil Fisher taught literature at the women's college across the river. Because of that, all he could talk about was women. Women this, women that. He thought most women were very spiritual.

Earl said, "You think my Sheila is spiritual? Running off with that French professor?"

"Maybe not your wife," Cecil said. "Sheila might not be all that spiritual."

"What do any of us really know about women?" I said. "Sure, some are spiritual. But others can be pretty carnal."

"Also sentimental," Cecil said. "I hate that."

"Then there's your bitches and your prickteasers," Earl said.

"All the way from Martha Stewart to Martha Theresa," I said. "Just kidding."

Earl said, "Cecil, how can you be so romantic about women after Vicki put all that windshield wiper solvent in your Chardonnay?"

"My wife might be another exception," Cecil said.

He poured himself another glass. He shook his head. "She slipped a cog. She didn't think I'd notice, could you believe it? I'm no connoisseur. I'm pretty lowbrow, you might say. But you tend to notice. You tend to notice those things, especially in your late vintage semi-sweets with the crisp finish."

"We need some women," I said. I poured the last of the wine into my glass and waggled the bottle. "We need to go somewhere. Not the faculty club, though."

"I know a place," Cecil said. He got up from the table. "That's where we'll go. To this place I know about."

Earl said. "In Hatfield? Off Montague Road? That place?"

"One of the strippers is taking my Wordsworth class," Cecil said. "That's how I know about it. How do you know about it?"

Club Castaway's outdoor sign said it had 40 girls available for entertaining. It didn't say whether they were all available at the same time. The inside was dark except for a floodlit stage, where a girl was dancing with a brass pole. She locked her legs around it. She slid her hands up and down it. She thrust her pelvis at it in time to the music.

In a corner of the bar, one girl looked different from the others. She had a few rolls of fat around her middle. She wore heavy make-up and a blonde wig. She sat on a guy's lap, facing him. She held onto his shoulders as she squirmed around, kicking her chubby legs out, forward and sideways.

"Ada Comstock Scholar," Cecil said. "There's probably a few more in the back. They get grants to go back to college when they're in their forties and fifties. They're called 'nontraditional' strippers."

He picked up his glass.

"They look unsafe," Earl said. "I mean, your diseases and all."

"They get a lot of action," Cecil said. "Fifty bucks for a lap dance. Two hundred you get to go into one of the back rooms. They can pay down their student loans pretty fast."

We were getting a little drunk. It was hard keeping things in focus. Earl and Cecil were ignoring the strippers. They began arguing over the etymology of "G-string." They didn't even notice when the lights flickered and a voice rumbled, "LADIES AND GENTLEMEN! CLUB CASTAWAY IS PROUD TO INTRODUCE ITS NEWEST STAR--- SHEILA THE PEELER."

The stripper came out. She had her back to us. She tossed her head from side to side and snapped her fingers. I watched her for awhile. She turned slightly toward us and twirled her tassels. She moved in a small circle in the middle of the stage

Earl and Cecil had their backs to her. They were talking about Earl's new book that he wrote *Intelligent Design for Dummies*. I had to give him a nudge.

"Look up there."

He turned around on his stool. He looked up at the stage. He blinked his eyes.

At the break, Sheila came over to our table. She held her robe closed at her throat. We were drinking Pernod and cream soda. She sat down. The bottle went around the table.

Earl went, "Honey, this can't continue. This has got to stop."

Sheila went, "Honey, stripping is killing me, too. But I didn't leave you. You left me." She nodded toward Cecil and me. "God," she went. "Always God. No time for me. Just God. God this, God that." Her eyes turned back to Earl. "You didn't love me. You only loved God, God damn you."

"Honey," Earl went, "It only lasted a month. It didn't mean anything. What about your French professor? What do you have to say about that?"

"Quand un jour d'hiver, comme je rentrais a la maison," she went, "ma mere me propose de me faire prendre..."

"Honey?"

...un peu de the. Elle envoya a chercher un de ces gateaux court..." she went.

"Honey?"

"...et dodus appelés Petites Madeleines qui semblant..." she went.

"Honey, should you be quoting Proust in a place like this?"

"Should you be wearing a clerical collar in a place like this, honey?"

"Should you be wearing nothing, honey?"

Cecil nodded toward me, "They're at it again."

Back on I-91, Cecil opens it up --- little jumps of eighty-five and ninety. Sheila and Earl are in the back seat. We're drinking Teachers and prune juice. The bottle goes around the car.

Sheila goes, "You understand? I'm only coming home with you because of the children. I want to see the children."

Earl goes, "The children? I thought you had the children, honey. Anyway, they'll turn up. Right now what counts is you and me. This is a serious matter we're discussing, honey. How can we get it right between you and me? We're talking human interaction here. Yours and mine"

"Human interaction, shit," she goes. "I'm trying to quit. You know that thing about icebergs, honey? One eighth above water, seven eighths underwater? Both ends are cold, honey. The top eighth is cold, the bottom seven eighths are cold, too."

Earl scratches his head like he's missed a boat. "Anyway, I want you to promise me something." He goes, "Honey, I want you to promise me you'll stop dancing in that shithole nightclub with those crazy Ada Comstock scholars."

"Be serious," she goes. "Besides, they're not girls. They're women. It is really insulting to call those women girls. I want to puke. They are women, honey."

"Not there they're not."

"Let s/he who is without sin," she goes, "let him/her throw up the first stone."

"Honey, how can we make it right between you and me? What does it take," he goes.

"How about fifty bucks for a lap dance," she says, "and two hundred for the back room, honey?"

Earl's face crumples. Tears roll off his cheeks. He dabs at his eyes with a handkerchief. Sheila's eyes roll upward, and then she puts her arm around his neck and draws him to her.

She goes, "Dos cuerpos por una sola miel derrotados."

"Honey," he sniffs, "honey, should you be quoting Neruda at a time like this?"

"Sure, honey. Neruda is saying, 'love is like two bodies subdued by honey'"

"That's us, honey."

"It's just about love, honey. Nothing personal."

This Can't Be Sunday

This can't be Sunday.
Last week we halted the *New York Times*,
With its inexorable
Absorption in God's solemn creation.
Nothing can linger but anger now.

What is Sunday
Without the *New York Times*?
Slow mornings
Soft bodies beneath the blankets
Kindhearted cups of coffee,
Wallpaper instead of newspaper,
Trips to the bakery and warm donuts
To balance the mind.

No news to soil our fingers
No ink stained bulletins to the brain.
We must once again
Attend church as we did in childhood
And pray for the sugar,
That soothes the spirit.
That sooths our soul,
Our essence, our fundament.

There is no more Sunday

Sugaring

As ants to vicious teens
Whiskey is to time
As the slurry light of an old barn
Glamorous maple
Is to my syrupy repose.
In the primitive landscape
Of my head
It's time to sugar daddy off

Odd Ode

These trees cascading,
this clump of shrubs
bowed and flashing
under the fierce pulsate pelt of rain
hasten grace and
stir my amygdala
to flow with associations.

O rostral anterior cingulate cortex,
aware of my optimistic
illusions, protect me
while I dream of faith.

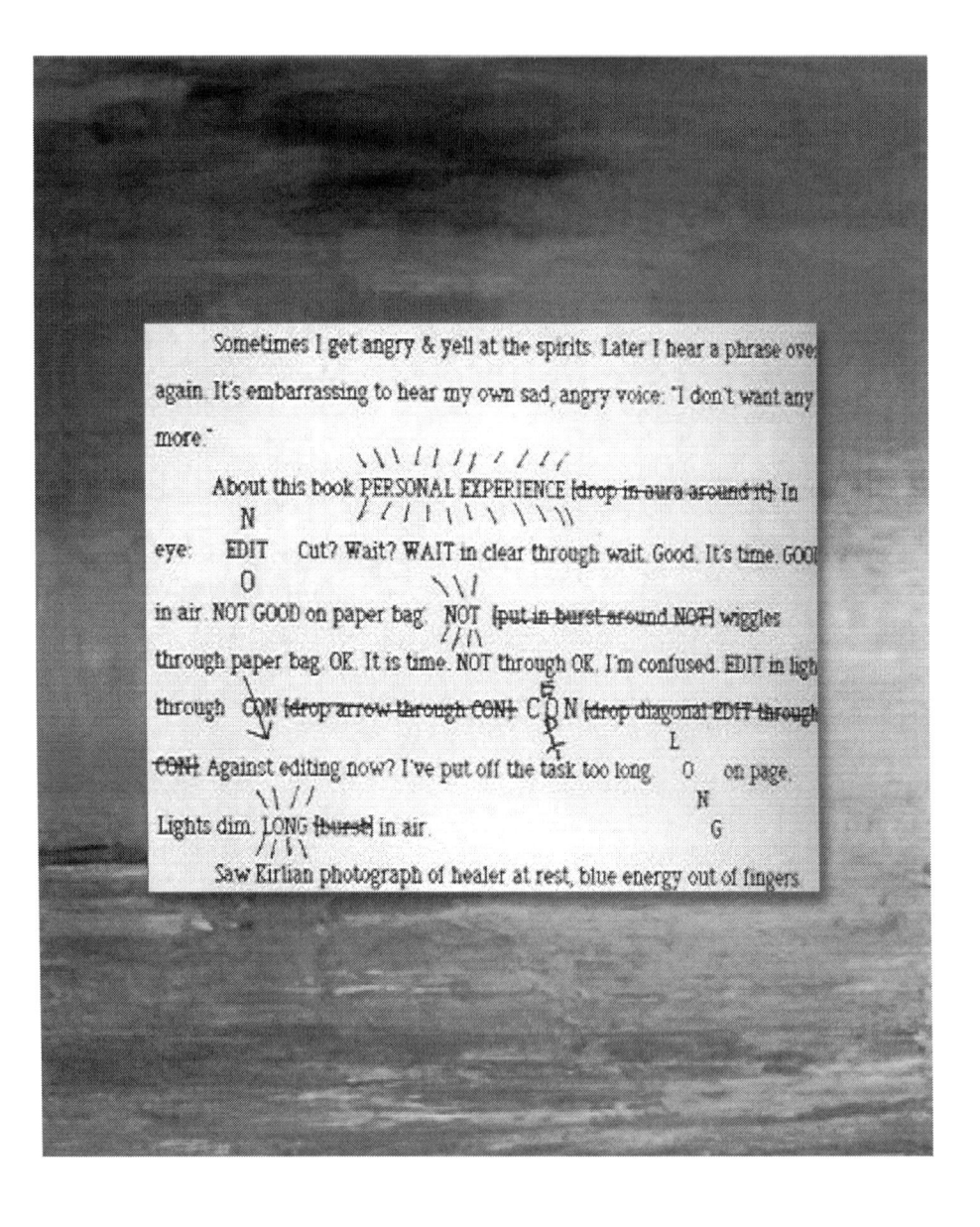

Sometimes I get angry & yell at the spirits. Later I hear a phrase over again. It's embarrassing to hear my own sad, angry voice: "I don't want any more."

About this book PERSONAL EXPERIENCE [drop in ours around it] In
N
eye: EDIT   Cut? Wait? WAIT in clear through wait. Good. It's time. GOO
O
in air. NOT GOOD on paper bag.   NOT [put in burst around NOT] wiggles
through paper bag. OK. It is time. NOT through OK. I'm confused. EDIT in ligh
through   CON [drop arrow through CON] C   N [drop diagonal EDIT through
L
CON] Against editing now? I've put off the task too long.   O   on page.
N
Lights dim. LONG [burst] in air.   G

Saw Kirlian photograph of healer at rest, blue energy out of fingers

Liver

Your liver has just arrived from California, Dad
  I see the helicopter outside
Churning on the hospital roof
  Bearing the fresh and steaming organ
Direct from whatever catastrophe
It was rescued.
  What sacrifice! What elation to set off
From a departed intellect
  A liver greater than the sum of its body's parts, with progressive installations to
  Feed unending beneficiaries
While its legatees feed it in return

Let those livers live in
 Us from
 Us in time
 In time
How cold these reflections are,
How unwillingly they leave my mouth.

Barista

Coffee is a short nod
To Helen, lurking
At the counter,
Handsome as a
Tortoise casing.
She conjures lattes
With the rhythm of
A joyful masque
For our suckling.
The froth's brash spirit
Jet Skis across each cup's surface

From foams of her youth
Is put into our paper cups to enclose us
In the music of tomorrow's wind
Swirling in exuberant breaths.
A silhouette lingers

Hot coffee slowly
Inch one-half minute no cause
Freedom catered to the growing

Tuesday At Ten For Health Insurance

She says she'll arrive
On time, thanks to an implausible device
that will position us globally.
Her GPS will know where to find me, and perhaps
Recognize me when it sees me,

She'll be coming not to examine me
but to give me the thing she has for me
my health insurance application
What health? Very few things
Propagate anymore in my body, and yet
My liver is still burstingly
Fertile --- its lobes and ducts send biles,
running sweetly, sweetly as a
fish-fattened freshet.

The health insurance
Application rests on her lap
she'll look down at it with tears in her eyes,
Still sipping
from the saucer of milk I set out for her.

Liberal Fascism

It began when Jonah found a
Whale right on page 36
At the bottom of screech
So Jonah Goldberg slept
with the whale
And brought him smoothing into
Anne Sexton's dead harbor.
Says Melville
Any fish can swim near the surface,
But it takes a great whale to go down
Stairs five miles or more; Jonah
From down below,
Saith his book: Social security and
medicare are "fascist," while Hitler,
being a vegetarian, was a liberal,
and Heinrich Himmler tended a garden
and raised chickens
hence a Green Activist.
Jonah saith "I believe God created the great whales,
and each Soul living, which maketh me a liberal
Along with the rest of them."

Bears On The Street

Its share price sinking
At implausible speed,
Vladalisco Company refocuses on
Its balance sheet.

Cut the rate of growth?
Cut the common stock?
Sell convertible preferred
to private firms?

Vladalisco ----has never missed
A quarterly earnings target.
"We don't have an earnings problem,"
Says the C.E.O.
"We have a multiples problem."

No one knows what he's talking about
And they are suspicious
That Vladalisco overpaid to
Acquire Big Bear Financial,

A company whose granaries
Once burst with bonds, derivatives,
And collateralized hypothocations
Piled to the rafters.

Now bears darken the night, and by day they
dance in the streets. Contrary to popular images,
bears are timid and prefer to eat in the woods unless we put out
honey. Says the C.E.O.. "Vladalico's merits have been overlooked
because of all these bears spreading one ridiculous rumor after
another."

Woman On An Island

Brave rays
      once left the slope of her hand,
hoping to radiate out into the stratosphere
      a clear signal
to those who wanted her.
But suns set, she knows,
Constellations fade, she knows, and
      in the end her weary rays
Flicker across the desert sea,
Lose their nerve, grow listless
While huddled masses,
those who were once necessary
      no longer are.

Smash and grab a sovereign state,
and her dark fire splutters, casting
      only shadows.
It's getting so you have
      to slap her awake
to face the nice girl
      she used to be.

STRIDENT LIGHT

The eye held clear
against the atmosphere, the
light
browsing across the sky
horizontal folios
printed dates
pressed
into lines of stability
info@simileimaging.com

For Felony, A Departed Cat

What was the matter with life on my shoulder?
Showing our scratches with rueful delight,
You had to thresh out your breath that much bolder,
Creeping away from the car in the night.
None of us noticed your silent departure,
Tending your terrors you ramble in dread,
And saunter along through my mind's dreamy summer,
Back to this room where the claws mark the bed.

Lifting Snowfall

Today we awake
to an anarchy of snow, and see
Under the window
the garden vanished,
the library smothered,
the parking lot lost beneath the soundless drifts.

Shoveling, I look down my nose at the snow,
the snow sneers back, white as a linen tablecloth
at the Copley Plaza, supercilious as that white
triturate which, released into the brain,
Freshly obliterates the molecules of memory
and the dark thoughts they inspire.

Scissors Confiscated In An Airport Line

From their forgotten hollow pocket in my backpack they must have loomed on the x-ray like angry birds of prey or the crossed swords of Zorro that could hack their way through blood and flame and treachery. Detached from my careless fingers their tininess was no excuse, although they'd snipped no more than a few threads, some chives from a windowsill pot, and ribbons on gifts for newlyweds, Christmas kids and birthday girls. Like many memories gone forever they were both innocent and lacerating.

Hallowe'en Afternoon

A small town, the store windows
Decorated with gravestones,
Witches, pumpkins,
Ghosts
Paint
        Streaking down
                The glass
                        In the rain.
A little girl dressed as
A rabbit, led across the street
By her mother,
Under an umbrella.
Have you ever stopped
To listen to the rain
In the lapse of a quarrel?
It means the quarrel will end.
It means you can see
The pavement on which the rain falls, and
The complexity of wet leaves
On it, curved leaves,
Flattened leaves.
The girl dressed as a rabbit
And her mother
Stop in front of an old
House with red shutters.
A chicken opens the door.

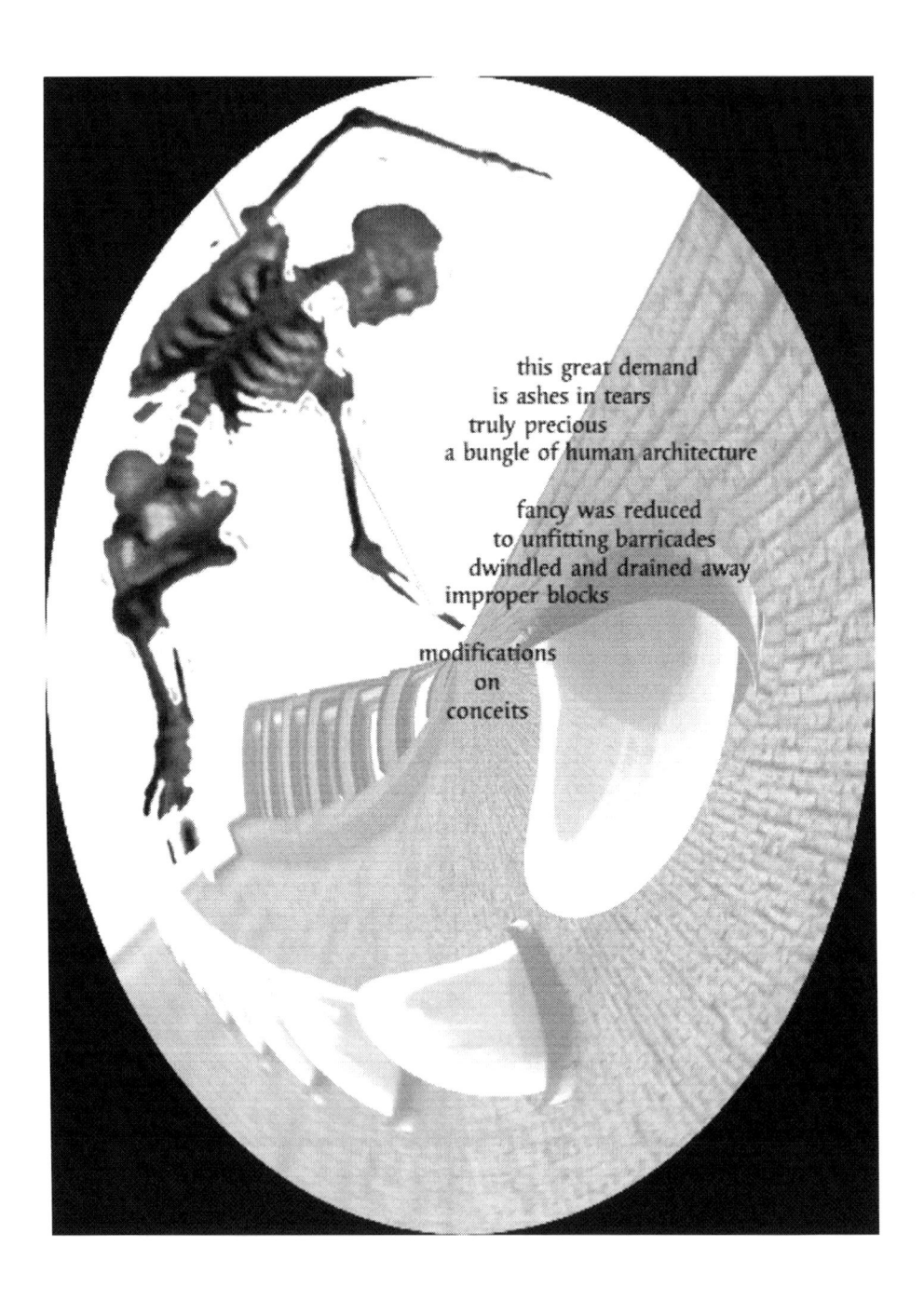

this great demand
is ashes in tears
truly precious
a bungle of human architecture

fancy was reduced
to unfitting barricades
dwindled and drained away
improper blocks

modifications
on
conceits

Mockingbird

Do not start with,
"If May is the month of the mockingbird,
September is the season of the dove."

After you have not written this,
take a break. Check mail. Delete message
from the ousted African Prince
who wants to deposit his fortune into your
bank account for safekeeping.

If they ask you where you've published,
say your poetry is "forthcoming."
Try an epithalamium—"for Rich & Sarah"—
Good for pulling you out of a slump.
Start, "If May is the month of the mockingbird,
September is the season of the dove."
Click on Marla Meehan, who wants to "increase your size"
(she never answers your e-mails). Select a poem
in a language you don't know
and write a translitic (verde = bare day).
Make a list of everything in your house
that is solitary, cold, and contemplative
including yourself. Change the font and write
a long letter protesting a parking ticket.
It should begin, "If May is the month of the mockingbird…"
There you go, it's starting to come.
You're waking up from your life.

Bobby Bear Ruins A Picnic

Bobby Bear had served as C.E.O. of many corporations, mostly in the food industry. His empire included Master Mustard and Madonna-style ketchup. He found lucrative markets in limes, lemons, Norwegian crackers, lard, apples, toilet paper and granola --- the kind of commodities that outdoor vacationers leave behind when their campsites are invaded by wild animals and they have to run away.

I did not know him well, but I had assisted him on a few deals over the years, mostly helping him to his competitors. He was now in middle age and had enjoyed 25 years of honest drinking and psychotherapy, both of which matched his four marriages. Wives two and four were the same person. Norma was a singer when he married her the first time. The second time around she had become an Exxon heiress.

Everything was going well for him. His stocks were soaring; he lunched regularly at the Knickerbocker Club and dined at Le Bernardin. His ghost-written memoir *Affluence and Ecstasy, the Era of Bobby Bear* had become a best seller.

Then, one day, he called me from Rockefeller University Hospital. He was having health problems. His nose bled. He sweated at night. It seemed that he had developed serious allergies to the products he had been merchandising over the years. The hospital had tried, at his insistence, transfusions of LSD, peyote, and garlic salt, all from companies in which he had a controlling interest. Nothing worked.

"I'm a goner," he told me. "They've been injecting me with the same kind of crap that you would find in the worst Post-punk vegetarian kitchens. They tell me I've only got six months. I need your advice."

"Well," I said, "now's the time to start communicating, to start saying goodbye at the gut level."

"Sure, okay, okay, yes, but I'd like to go out with pride. There are a few transactions I'd like to close before the end of the six months. You can help. Only you."

He described some of his ambitions: There was a fracking job in Chicago, starting under the loop and extending south along Lake Shore Drive. The aldermen were pretty well lined up. He wanted to dope some more baseball players, down to the still-wide-open Little Leagues. There was a porno deal with North Korea, but the government wanted a piece of the action that would include missile sites.

"I'm not sure I can help you," I said, not without admiration. "These are going to be big promos."

Yes, and here's one right up your pattootie. We're calling it the "Consensual Coffin." I got the idea right here at the hospital and my guys are working on it, which is why I need you. Lets say $10,000 gets the buyer into the coffin. With the family's consent they bury him, face down. He lies in it for awhile. On the third day he rises from the dead. Absolute guarantee. You like it? I'll cut you in 50-50."

"I don't know," I told him. "It doesn't quite fit my business plan."

His laughter ended with a snort. "Everybody has a price, right? So sit down and let's talk. First, throw back that hood. I don't deal with anyone unless there's eye contact. Second, get rid of that gray outfit... the suit... robe...whatever it is... ."

"Okay. But what do I do with the scythe?"

"Janitor's closet next to the operating room. This deal could be a messy."

Bunny

Sarah was four years old. She had a mother, a father, a brother named Peter, and a pet lop-eared bunny.

They all lived in a fine old house surrounded by lilacs and rhododendrons. Sarah's mother sometimes cut the flowers and arranged them in a Ming Dynasty vase that she kept on a table in the front hall.

In Sarah's room, the rabbit's cage rested on the floor beside her big, brass bed. A large table stretched the length of the room, and on the table were stacks of coloring books, crayons, pebbles, seagull feathers, glue, and a pair of scissors—all the things Sarah needed for her projects. Working at these projects was her idea of a fine time. Her window faced the backyard, and the late afternoon sun streamed across her desk as she worked.

One day, Sarah's mother came up behind her and asked her to clean up her work table. The light from the afternoon sun was slanting across the pebbles and the seagull feathers at just the right angle, spreading like warm honey across her drawings and her scrapbook. The rabbit was curled up in his cage, a half-eaten carrot lying next to his outstretched ear.

"I'm busy," Sarah said. She looked down at the bunny, whose nose was twitching. "I'm very, very busy," she repeated.

"But you really must clean up your table, dear," Sarah's mother said. "And then it will be time for your bath."

"I'm too busy for a bath," Sarah said.

"But dear," we all have to wash ourselves from time to time."

"Get out of my house!" Sarah said.

"Oh, dear," said her mother. She retreated into the hallway and closed the door behind her.

Soon, her father and brother appeared. "Sarah," her father said, "it's time for your bath, and please apologize to your mother."

"Get out of my house!" Sarah said.

Peter, her brother, said, "Will you please stop cutting up the shoelaces from my sneakers and pasting them in your scrapbook?"

"Get out of my house" Sarah said.

"Oh, my, oh my, oh," said her father and Peter, as they stepped back into the hallway and closed the door behind them.

Sarah thought, "This house would be perfect except for one thing. There are too many bossy people living in it." Sarah continued to work on her project. She made a puddle of glue in the middle of a piece of paper, and into it she pushed pieces of her brother's shoelace, a seagull feather, and a cherry lifesaver. The rabbit snored contentedly.

After a while, Sarah heard the sound of footsteps. She opened the door a crack and looked down the back stairs. She saw her father emerging from the basement, where he kept his dim and dreary workshop. He had a large sack over his shoulder and a hammer in his hand. Next came Sarah's mother, carrying a metal box and a sharp, long-handled fork. Then came Peter, carrying some cloth bags and a long piece of rope. They were carrying all the tools up from the workshop.

Sarah continued to glue and paste.

A while later, Sarah looked down into the backyard. She could see her father driving small pegs into the ground with his hammer, while her brother unfolded the tent. Her mother was cooking hot dogs on the charcoal grill, turning them with the long-handled fork. The sleeping bags lay unrolled next to the picnic table.

"Good," Sarah said to herself, as she pressed a few pebbles into the puddle of glue. The light through the window had never been clearer, nor the objects on her desk more enticing. She cleaned up the materials on her work table, putting each object in its proper place.

Then she went into the bathroom and ran herself a tub of deliciously hot water. As she warmed herself in the bath, she stared drowsily at the ceiling. Soon she fell asleep and dreamed about rocks with seagulls circling over them on the shore of an ocean. All the tools from the workshop, hammers and saws, drills and chisels, were dancing joyfullyarm in arm across the rocky beach.

When she awoke, raindrops were streaking the bathroom window. Wrapping herself in a towel, she returned to the bedroom. The tent in the backyard below was glistening in the rain. The charcoal in the portable grill had turned into a thick, black puddle. No one was in sight.

"Good," Sarah said to herself.

She threw an old blanket over her shoulders and went downstairs to the kitchen. She opened the refrigerator, found some cold food, and ate it quickly. It was tasteless. "Things are different now," she told herself.

She took a handful of carrots upstairs for the rabbit who was looking hungry and forlorn.

"Don't be sad, my bunny, she told him. "Now we have this fine house all to ourselves, with no one to boss us around. Go to sleep now."

The next morning, the doorbell rang. It was Mr. Eames, the postman. Sarah hurried downstairs, pulling the blanket around her shoulders.

"Good morning, miss," he said. "I have a special letter here. Will you sign for it?"

Sarah did as she was told, signing her name as best she could, with the "S" backwards and the "h" upside down.

"What does it say?" she asked.

Mr. Eames held the envelope up to the light. "It seems that someone in your family has won a prize."

"Hooray," said Sarah, clapping her hands.

"And all you have to do," Mr. Eames continued, "is visit a place called El Encanto By-the-Sea, Vacation Townhomes, to pick up your prize."

"Oh," said Sarah, disappointed. "You see, my family has run away from home. I wouldn't know how to get there by myself."

"Cheer up," said Mr. Eames. "I could give you a ride in my mail truck, after work. I could do that. I'd love to see what you've won. And I'd love to visit any place with a name like El Encanto By-the-Sea."

Sarah was delighted. She wanted to smother his neck with kisses, but Mr. Eames smiled quickly and backed down the front steps.

Sarah put the letter into a wire basket that rested on the front hall table next to the Ming vase. She wished that there were someone who could read the letter to her, read it over and over.

She went upstairs and decided to let the rabbit out of his cage. This was not allowed when her mother and father were in the house. Sarah found some pink ribbon in her mother's sewing kit and tied it firmly around the rabbit's neck. She laughed as he hopped in circles around the legs of her work table. Then he scurried away under the big, brass bed.

The doorbell rang again.

Two men, dressed in black suits, were standing on the front porch. One of them held a black briefcase. Sarah was not sure if she should let them in, but she did.

"Good morning, little miss," said one of the men. His black hair was closely cropped and when he smiled Sarah noticed that a front tooth was missing. "Are you the lady of the house?"

Sarah said that she was the lady of the house.

"Well, then," said the man, handing her a pamphlet, "have you accepted Jesus Christ as your lord and savior?"

Sarah was not quite sure.

"Well, you'd better," the second man scowled, "and you'd better do it fast." But the first man shushed him.

"Little lady," said the first, "this is our newspaper. Can you read?"

"Of course," said Sarah bravely.

"Well, read it. Read the first paragraph."

Sarah looked at the pamphlet, but all she could see was a picture of a lighthouse, and letters, some of which she recognized, but most of which made no sense.

"She's lying," said the second man. "She can't read a word of the Holy Writ." He stepped forward with his fist raised, but the first man held him back, with a hand on his stomach.

"Easy, Ralph, don't get carried away by the gentle words of Our Blessed Savior," he said. "Tell me, little miss, why did you say that you could read?"

Sarah began to cry.

"Why are you here all alone, little lady?"

She could not answer. She just shook her head as more tears came.

"Look at that vase," Ralph said. "Nice vase." He stroked it with his hand. He patted the edges

"Easy, Ralph," said the first man. "There, there, little lady. Don't cry. The world is full of wonderful people, even though some of them are liars." He patted Sarah's shoulder. "We won't tell anyone you were untruthful about being able to read, if only we could have some of the beautiful flowers in that vase, to share with others less fortunate then yourself."

"They're yours," Sarah sobbed.

The second man picked up the Ming vase. "Bet they've got silver back there in a pantry drawer, Chief."

"No, Ralph, no," said the first man. "This little lady has been most generous already. Let us thank her, and then we'll be on our way."

He tossed a cheerful smile-with-the-missing-tooth at Sarah. "For the beauty of the earth," he said by way of parting. The two men backed down the front steps, turned, and walked slowly down the sidewalk, holding the vase with the flowers in it. When they reached the big maple tree by the driveway, they began to run.

Sarah returned to her bedroom and found that the room was dim. The rabbit had eaten through the electrical cords and the telephone wire. Her crayons, pebbles and seagull feathers had been knocked off the table, and disgusting brown pellets were strewn across the floor.

"Bad bunny," said Sarah. "Bad, bad bunny."

The rabbit sat on the bed, twitching his ears. His two narrow eyes, one on each side of his head, faced in opposite directions, but Sarah knew, as he squinted at her, that he could see her through both of them. His nose twitched. He opened his mouth and made a throaty noise that sounded like, "GEDD ...OUD...OVV...MYEE...HOU---ZZE...." Sarah shrieked and ran down the stairs.

There, at the front door, were her father, her mother, and her brother, crowded together and smiling. Sarah was so glad to see them she almost fainted.

"Could we borrow a cup of sugar?" said her mother. She was holding an empty paper cup.

"Come in, come in," said Sarah in a quavering voice. "We have lots of sugar."

Sarah's family came through the front door. Her mother looked around as if she were visiting the house for the first time. At first, she did not seem to notice the empty space on the front hall table. Then she frowned at it, searching her mind.

They all crowded together in the kitchen, and Sarah opened the drawers below the counter until they formed a ladder. She climbed up on them, knelt on the counter, and reached into the cupboard next to the sink. Then she carefully poured the sugar from its box into her mother's paper cup.

"Would you like some tea with your sugar?" Sarah asked.

"Oh, heavens no," said her mother.

"We really have to be going," said her brother.

"But thanks for asking," said her father.

The family filed out of the kitchen, laughing together. At the front door, her father turned. "It's nice to have a good neighbor like you," he said, "who gives us her sugar." And then they were gone.

Later that evening, with the rabbit scampering through the house knocking over furniture and gnawing at things, Sarah sat at the window of her locked bedroom, hugging herself beneath the blanket.

Below, she could see her family in the backyard. They were in their pajamas. Mother was kneeling on the grass, washing the dinner dishes in a plastic tub. Father was reading to Peter by the light of a Coleman lantern. After a while, they all crawled into the tent, except for her father. He took out the hammer from his workshop and nailed a few more boards onto the new fence he was building across the lawn to separate them from the house. Then he turned down the lantern flame, and there was only darkness, the sound of crickets, and the sound of a bunny munching on wallpaper.

"This is the way it will be, then," Sarah thought to herself. "I will grow up in a family of neighbors. Just neighbors. No more family."

Soon she was asleep, by herself, in the old house that she liked so much, dreaming of hammers and nails, seagulls and rocks.

But she didn't know, how could she? There on her front doorstep, there in the darkness, sat Mr. Eames, the postman. He was smoking a cigar, still wearing his gray uniform. He had left the motor running in his mail truck. He was waiting; he was waiting to take her to El- Encanto-By-the-Sea.

Where was she?

Up North

He'd come to Northern Michigan, and the lake gulls were shrieking at him. He'd been on vacation only two days, but he sat around the cabin, springing up now and then to go to the window and back. It was too chilly to go out onto the beach. The sky looked like rumpled tinfoil and the wind was strong and cold. Lake Superior came rolling up to the beach with thundering splashes.

He would go to the door, then return and slump by the fire. I also heard him last night, walking around upstairs in the night, mumbling swear words in the darkness.

This morning he fidgeted around the cabin for an hour, not eating anything.

"Demon," he said. "No, that's not it."

Lucy, my sister, had wrapped a blanket around her. She shivered and looked out the window. "Demeanor," our father said. He laughed quickly and without sparkle, "No, that's not the word."

"Don't worry about it, Dad," I said, "The word isn't important."

Lucy said, "Dad, I can tell you the word."

"No, no," our father said. He held up his hand. "I've almost got it."

"Demeanor," he said. He shook his head.

We first noticed it last year when we drove up here. We stopped at a gas station. He put his wallet on the roof of the car while he filled the tank. Later, he said, "It was the credit card." The words on the gas pump flustered him --- remove card rapidly.

We drove off with the wallet still on the roof. We didn't discover the loss until we arrived here three hours later.

"Debilitate," he says. "Dyslexia."

"Dad, cut it out," Lucy says, "you're making us crazy."

"Crazy," he says.

The waves sweep along the shore.

"Dementia!" he says suddenly. "That's it! Dementia. That's the word the doctor used. Comes just before Alzheimer's. Remember? Do you remember?"

"Dad," I say, "don't worry. The doctor said it could be a long way off. It doesn't happen right away."

Our father straightens himself before the window, watching the waves.

"A long way off," he says.

He says, "Please keep helping me to remember...help me to keep remembering... the word."

Made in the USA
Lexington, KY
30 December 2014